201

Studymates

British History 1870–1918
Warfare 1792–1918
Hitler and Nazi Germany (3rd Edition)
English Reformation
European History 1870–1918
Genetics (2nd edition)
Lenin, Stalin and Communist Russia
Organic Chemistry (2nd Edition)
Chemistry: As Chemistry Explained
Chemistry: Chemistry Calculations Explained
The New Science Teacher's Handbook
Mathematics for Adults
Calculus
Understanding Forces
Algebra: Basic Algebra Explained
Plant Physiology
Poems to Live By
Shakespeare
Poetry
Better English
Better French
Better German
Better Spanish
Social Anthropology
Statistics for Social Science
Practical Drama
The War Poets 1914–18
The Academic Essay
Your Master's Thesis
Your PhD Thesis

Studymates
Helping You to Achieve

Your PhD Thesis

University of Nottingham
at Derby Library

Robert Brewer

Contents

Author's Preface

Here is an authoritative guide, which provides extensive advice on many aspects of the process of obtaining a PhD or other doctorate. It covers a variety of topics from identifying a research question or hypothesis and an appropriate research paradigm and method through to dealing with the difficulties of presentation, layout, referencing and bibliography. It constitutes not only a readily accessible introduction to the task but a source of reference, which can usefully be kept to hand during the field research, and the process of writing up. It must be emphasised that this is not a book on research methods. Rather, it seeks to place research methods within the context of the research process as a whole from an initial consideration of the nature of research to the final submission of the thesis.

Readers may need to be aware of developments that are under discussion in the United Kingdom. The Quality Assurance Agency for England, Wales and Northern Ireland has engaged in consultations that have led to the positioning of postgraduate qualifications within the National Qualifications Frameworks. While the PhD/D.Phil is not proposed for credit rating nor would it be achievable by credit accumulation; nevertheless, institutions may require students to undertake assessed and credit-rated courses (e.g. in research methods) prior to or during their studies.

Some doctorates may be achievable by credit accumulation including taught modules, professional or practice-based work and research elements. These include the professional doctorates such as those in Engineering, Education, Clinical Psychology and Business Administration, and more titles are developing which define more precisely the area of the award. It is likely that the research elements in these degrees will need to be seen as comparable in standard if not in scale, with that of the supervised PhD. The 'New Route PhD', while requiring some taught elements to develop a sufficient breadth of subject knowledge to meet the criticism that the traditional PhD is too narrowly focused, will still require research of the same standard as the traditional PhD (UK Council for Graduate Education, 2002).

None of these developments is likely in the foreseeable future to diminish the significance of the issues treated in this book.

Professor Robert Brewer
r.brewer@studymates.co.uk

1 The Nature of Research

One-minute overview

Research is essentially derived from the needs and practices of everyday life. It fulfils the purposes of describing, examining, explaining and developing new ideas. In academic terms, it may develop or test theory, describe existing knowledge or solve specific problems. Doctoral work is often characterised by the compromise between the high level of originality offered by the first two, and the greater likelihood of success offered by the latter two. Research is pursued by different individuals for a variety of reasons, including the need to solve problems, acquire information, advance a career, or simply out of interest. Whatever the reasons, there are always problems surrounding how to begin and how to write up, and these form the focus of this book. Doctoral work may also be pursued for a variety of reasons, but there are also good reasons not to undertake such a task and these need to be weighed in the balance before commencing. The essential features of a doctorate must also be considered, as well as the various ways in which a PhD may make an authoritative original contribution. This involves acquiring the necessary 'craft skills' in order to demonstrate your credentials as a professional researcher.

Most of us undertake research in some form or another nearly every day of our lives. We all, at some point, need to find information we do not know but suddenly need, for example in order to plan a holiday or business journey. This represents a wide view of research in that it enables us to lead our lives with greater effectiveness. More narrowly, research may tell us that there is something we do not know (as opposed to telling us *about* something we do not know) or that the information we thought we had is incorrect – for example, the exact date on which some event important to us occurred. This kind of research can often bring us up short, forcing us to perhaps question long-held views and positions, refocus our thinking, and adjust to a new and perhaps more complex reality.

It can be seen therefore that research may have a number of different purposes.

1. Description – what is the situation? What is the problem exactly? What has happened or is happening?
2. Examining critically the current state of knowledge.
3. Explanation – analysing why particular situations exist.
4. Development of new constructs or theories.

Research may also be classified by the way it contributes to our knowledge. It may:

1. develop pure theory;
2. test existing theory;
3. describe existing knowledge;
4. solve specific problems.

As Grinyer (1981, quoted in Howard and Sharp, 1983:12–13) has suggested, in relation to the chances of the successful completion of a PhD, the bottom end of the list tends to increase the prospects of success, whereas the level of originality increases towards the top, together with the possibility of failure.

But why conduct research at all? It can, after all, be a complex, time-consuming and frustrating business. There are a number of possible answers or combination of answers:

1. purely out of interest – in order to find out more about something in which you are interested e.g. the biography of a particular individual;
2. you might need to meet the requirements of a degree or other course you are studying;
3. you may need information for a particular cause you support, e.g. on homelessness, in order to enable it to present a more effective case;

4. a business or technical problem may have to be solved e.g. developing or marketing a new product;
5. in order to be able to evaluate other people's research e.g. as presented in the press, on television or in academic journals;
6. in order to advance an academic career.

Many would-be researchers considering undertaking a piece of research for the first time see a number of possible problems:

1. Where to begin?
2. How long will it take?
3. What research methods should I use?
4. How do I record, store and analyse information?
5. How can I ensure the data I collect corresponds to the title of the research?
6. How do I write it all up?

This book will essentially deal with problems 1 and 6, together with some coverage of the elements that compose 2 and 3 in the list above.

It must be emphasised that this book is essentially about the preparatory and writing processes rather than a book about research and analytical methods. The research and analytical methods are dealt with elsewhere as indicated by the books in the Bibliography.

However, it is worth reiterating that the essentials of research are present in your everyday life. What is needed is to put these essentials into a systematic form in order to obtain reliable knowledge through observations – the basis of a scientific approach, and to develop ways of explaining your observations.

Why do a PhD?

There are many reasons. They include:

1. to make a significant and original contribution in your chosen field;
2. to pursue a particular interest.

3. to continue research previously started;
4. to develop career opportunities;
5. to become an acknowledged authority in your chosen field;
6. to become a professional researcher.

Why NOT to do a PhD.

1. You wish really to undertake another form of research activity e.g. you may wish to write a book for popular consumption.
2. Your research – interesting and important as it is to you – is not suitable for a PhD.
3. You do not wish to inflict on your family the necessary sacrifices.
4. You do not wish to engage in some of the seemingly frustrating and pointless activities involved.
5. The extrinsic benefits of a PhD do not outweigh the costs (of all kinds) – a PhD does not necessarily advance your career and may even hinder it!
6. To experience the pleasure of being called 'Dr'.
7. You lack the necessary determination and application to complete the job.
8. Being unable to think of an alternative career move.

To succeed you MUST

1. have the determination and drive to succeed in overcoming the troughs and despair which will inevitably accompany the process – brilliance is neither necessary nor sufficient;
2. realise that like any other job of work it has to be finished and completed within certain parameters of time and resources – which will involve various compromises along the way e.g. between time available and scope.

So you still want to do a PhD?

Then there are a number of things you need to do in the beginning.

1. Approach several convenient or otherwise suitable university institutions – by letter, telephone call, e-mail, the contact page on their website – to establish whether they have research interests in your field. Do not assume all universities have research interests in all possible fields or that they will necessarily have a suitable supervisor available. It can be disheartening to receive rejections not because you or your chosen topic area are unsuitable but because the universities in question do not have an appropriate supervisor e.g. in Chinese management.

2. Read the various postgraduate prospectuses for the institutions you are considering, to see what provisions they make in terms of supervision or courses in research methods, and the length of time allowed between registration (which may take place some time after you effectively commence work on your PhD depending on how long it takes to develop a suitable project) and submission (which may be quite some time before you are actually examined).

3. Make sure you understand the REQUIREMENTS for the PhD in the various institutions in which you are interested e.g. word length, possible requirements to attend certain courses, the format of presentation. While these may be broadly similar, there will be institutional variations, e.g. word limitations may vary not only from university to university but from faculty to faculty within universities.

You would not normally be expected to have a fully-fledged topic with research questions worked out at this stage, but you should have identified a topic area, have some idea of the research you wish to pursue within it, and be prepared to defend it and its value.

Assuming you are still determined to pursue doctoral research and that you have identified a university or universities willing to accept you, this may be the point at which to reconsider the essential features of the PhD.

1. It must have something worthwhile to say so that others will listen.
2. It must demonstrate a command of what is going on in this research area and evaluate what others have contributed or are contributing on a worldwide basis.
3. It must identify an area in which you can make an original contribution.
4. It must show an adequate mastery of the necessary research techniques involved and an understanding of their justification and limitations.
5. It must communicate the findings effectively and with due regard to the academic conventions surrounding publication.

It is important to remember that your PhD thesis will be available for others to read on the library shelves regardless of whether you publish in any other form.

A final word on the subject of originality and what constitutes an original contribution to knowledge. There are a number of ways in which a PhD can be original – they include the following.

1. Discovering new information.
2. Developing a new technique and demonstrating its application.
3. Making a new synthesis of existing data.
4. Applying an established technique in a new area.
5. Conducting new empirical work.
6. Developing a new research area.
7. Using an inter-disciplinary approach in an area where it has not been applied before.
8. Using a different methodology to examine an area previously investigated.

Doubtless there are also other ways in which the concept of originality can be demonstrated and ultimately much depends on the view of originality held by any individual examiner. Nevertheless, it is clear from the above list that it is only an incremental step in existing knowledge that is required – a small advance – not a paradigm shift. In the final analysis, while the criterion of the original contribution to knowledge remains the essential distinctive feature of the PhD, it should not continue to be the barrier to research progress that students may fear at the outset.

What is a PhD?

It can be many things. However, there are certain characteristics that are common to all doctoral theses.

1. It speaks with authority.
2. It makes a distinctive contribution.
3. It says something which is worth listening to.
4. It demonstrates an awareness of the context of the subject – internationally if appropriate.
5. It makes appropriate use of suitable research techniques with due regard to their limitations.
6. It communicates professionally the conclusions of the research.

Above all, these things have to be put together with due regard for 'academic craft'. This involves investigating and acquiring relevant skills – something which is not done overnight. The need for these skills underlines the role of the supervisor in ensuring access to the means of acquiring them both, directly – from the supervisor or lectures on research methods and related matters – and indirectly, from others in seminars, conferences and informal discussions.

The learning of the professional skills required by a PhD student also has to be accompanied by the supremely important ability (which may have to be acquired) to continuously reassess the value of the work he or she has done in the light of the work that is being done by others. This can be difficult and painful as it may involve the realization that their work has now acquired a different significance given new developments, or may simply have become irrelevant.

A PhD demonstrates the acquisition of the skills that make up 'academic craft' and entitle the researcher to be recognised as a professional. It is the badge that marks out the recognised professional researcher. This includes

1. the ability to conduct a mature review demonstrating comprehension of the difficult and complex material involved in the field of study;
2. learning which has taken place at the appropriate standard to enable the PhD holder to contribute further to research in their field of study without supervision and ultimately to be able to assist others to do the same (although not all PhD holders will wish to do this or will have the opportunity to do so).

In summary, a PhD

1. says something new or original;
2. shows grasp of a field of study;
3. displays the skills of 'academic craft';
4. does these things to a standard required of a professional researcher working independently.

Tutorial

Progress questions

1. How would you define research?
2. What do you think are the differences between research in everyday life and academic research?
3. What do you regard as the essential characteristics of the PhD?

Discussion points

1. Why do you wish to undertake a PhD?
2. Why might you NOT wish to undertake a PhD?

Practical assignments

1. Write down any research activity you have undertaken at the end of the day and assess its amount and importance to you.
2. Examine the research degree prospectuses in your public reference library or local university library; list the features the PhD programmes and regulations have in common and which are different, for several universities at which it might be feasible for you to consider registering.

Study and revision tips

1. Clarify in your own mind and write down the reasons why you want to pursue a PhD. These may change but the exercise will help you in any interview you may have with a potential supervisor.
2. Think about the broad area in which you are considering researching and justify why you think it is interesting and important to research in this area.

2   Types of Research

One-minute overview

Different fields of research tends to favour different approaches to research, and particular approaches may be regarded as conferring legitimacy and validity in particular fields. Whatever research method you choose to use may be open to challenge and so you need to be clear that the method needs to be conducted rigorously within the selected field of research. Acceptable research is likely to display the characteristics of an open examination of every facet of relevant thought, critical examination of evidence and the formulating of generalizations but within recognised limitations. Research is classified in various ways by different authors including exploratory, descriptive, analytical and predictive, each with its own purposes and characteristics. Many researchers also tend to have a natural affinity towards qualitative or quantitative approaches, the former being used in exploratory research, the latter in testing hypotheses. The two approaches may be used together in some approaches such as case studies, but in doing so the potential issues must be recognised.

Any investigator comes to a research project with a favoured approach with which they feel at ease. Approaches may include, for example, survey research of the public opinion variety, observational techniques as employed in studies of classroom behaviour, action research into organisational problems, archival studies of historical problems, interview methods employing content analysis, and scientific experiments involving hypothesis testing in a laboratory environment. Different fields of research tend to favour different approaches, and the acceptance of a particular approach may be important in conferring legitimacy upon the knowledge acquired as being valid.

Whatever approach is used, it must be remembered that the conclusions of the research are inevitably tentative and open to challenge.

The issues are:

- whether a completed piece of research has been conducted rigorously within its selected method,
- whether the choice of method was appropriate to the research question, and
- whether the study was firmly grounded on a suitable conceptual and theoretical basis.

The danger is that students will have been familiar with one approach to research and assume that this is applicable to all situations. The research method may, in effect, be chosen before the research question has been determined, regardless of whether it will appropriately address this question. It is the research question that must determine the range of methodological options available and thus significantly contribute to the final choice of method.

As indicated above, this is not a book about research methods, but it is helpful to place thinking about doing a research project for a PhD in the context of research methods without making any presumption about the primacy of any particular method or about the method that will ultimately be chosen. Whatever the method to be used, research which is likely to be acceptable will display certain characteristics.

1. The open examination of any and every facet of thought which is relevant to the research – nothing is excluded from critical evaluation no matter how established the knowledge reviewed or how conventional is the wisdom being tested through the application of appropriate theoretical frameworks.

2. Critical examination of evidence, including the quality of the data, its validity and reliability and the different interpretations that can be placed upon it.
3. A recognition of both the need to make valid generalisations and the limitations of these generalisations.

There are a number of ways in which research can be classified. Hussey and Hussey (1997) have suggested a typology whereby the basis of the classification rests upon the:

1. purpose of the research;
2. process of the research;
3. logic of the research;
4. outcome of the research.

Using the above framework, they go on to classify types of research in the following way.

Purposes of the research may involve the following types of research.

1. Exploratory
2. Descriptive
3. Analytical
4. Predictive

Process may refer to

1. quantitative or
2. qualitative techniques.

The logic of the research may involve

1. deductive or
2. inductive reasoning.

Outcome of the research may refer to

1. applied or
2. basic research.

Phillips and Pugh (1994) suggest a three-fold classification.

1. Exploratory
2. Testing-out
3. Problem-solving.

All three may involve either quantitative or qualitative methods, or both.

It may be worth considering these types of research in greater detail before examining their possible relationship to thinking abut a PhD research project. They constitute part of the context within which consideration of the possibility of undertaking a research project for a PhD may be placed.

Exploratory Research

This may be undertaken when insufficient is known about a particular problem, so that the current state of research does not permit the formulation of hypotheses. An exploratory study is therefore used in order to look for patterns or ideas that might lead to the establishment of an hypothesis that can be tested. The focus of an exploratory study is therefore on gaining more information and insights about a subject in order to pave the way for further, more rigorous, research. It should be noted that the problem involved may be theoretical or empirical and that the research will need to consider whether any

1. existing concepts or theories are useful and relevant, especially if suitably adapted;
2. new concepts or theories need to be developed;
3. established methods can fruitfully be employed.

The exploratory approach therefore typically involves case studies, participant or non-participant observational techniques, and collection and analysis of historical data, while quantitative and qualitative techniques, processes and data may be involved. Thus, a broad and flexible spectrum of techniques may be called upon, as it may be necessary to collect a wide range of material in a variety of different ways in order to provide some insight into possible relationships that may be worth further exploration, although at this stage conclusive answers are unlikely.

Exploratory research

The exploratory research approach to pursuing a PhD clearly, therefore, offers fairly readily the original contribution required to secure the degree. Nevertheless, the relatively unstructured nature the approach is likely to involve, the lack of benchmarks, and the difficulty of producing immediately publishable work may make it less attractive than it may seem. It is a relatively high-risk strategy that, if successful, may make your name and provide a basis for you to continue with the research. Alternatively, it may leave you floundering without a viable thesis to submit.

Descriptive research

This may take exploratory research a stage further. It provides a detailed account of the characteristics of some issue or phenomenon and may lead to some kind of labelling or sorting out which enables classification into categories. For example, if you were fortunate enough to discover the Loch Ness monster, you would initially have to describe its various characteristics, measurements etc and observe different aspects of its behaviour patterns in order to begin to attempt to place it in some genus or species, about which you would have to form an hypothesis. Some of this data may well be quantitative and involve the use of statistical procedures or at least statistical methods of presentation such as bar or pie charts. The approach often involves seeking answers to questions beginning with 'what'. What is the truancy rate among secondary school pupils in comprehensive schools in England? What feelings do office workers have about imminent retirement? What is the number of goals scored by players in midfield positions in football teams playing in the English Premier league over the last three football seasons?

In considering descriptive research it is important to note that the term can cover several different kinds of descriptive approach (Dunleavy, 2003).

1. Narrative – where a 'story' is told by the author such as may often be used in studies of literary criticism, for example, when Act 1 of a Shakespeare play is discussed, then Act 2, followed by Act 3 etc

2. Chronological – where an historical sequence in effect becomes the structure as is often the case in studies of historical events e.g. the reign of Henry VIII, or in biographies.

3. Organisational – where the structure of the thesis follows the structure of the organisation or institution, or the pattern of relationships between different organisations or institutions, or the structure of an Act of Parliament or a set of regulations or a statutory instrument. Clearly, this pattern is likely to be found in theses on Law, or Public and Social Administration.

Other forms of descriptive pattern can also be suggested, such as spatial organisation in studies of Geography (Dunleavy, 2003).

While using a descriptive approach to research is popular (and sometimes justified – as in the example of the Loch Ness monster quoted above) it can also be very harmful because

1. it requires a great many facts or a great deal of data in order to function adequately;

2. the very heavy load becomes difficult to organise.

This often makes the argument difficult for readers to comprehend and the themes and analysis become very difficult to disentangle. While the relative luxury of time and space may make the technique more operable at PhD than at lower levels, in fact a formidable level of writing skill is required. It is necessary to introduce and then in some way interlace into the texture of the extensive description the required conceptualisation for analytical purposes or the main lines of the argument. This is actually quite difficult. There are two main problems.

1. The argument underpinning the thesis becomes disorganised and disappears into a complex morass.

2. A particular organisational facet e.g. geographical or historical proximity, or personal or institutional relationships becomes the basis of the structure without necessarily being of any real significance in itself.

Theses that fall into either (or both) of these traps can then appear to be organisationally devoid of any internal or conceptual structure. It then becomes necessary to develop an analytical or argumentative explanation in order to make sense of the material.

Analytical research

This goes beyond descriptive research in that it attempts to explain the data described. It seeks to explain why things are as they are, or how they came to be as they are, by a process of analysis and explanation. It does this by looking for causal relationships amongst the data involved and attempting to measure them. One example might be the collection of information relating to the size of schools and the examination results of the pupils. Analytical research in education might attempt to answer such questions as:

How can the level of truancy on the part of pupils be reduced?

How can we expand the number of examination subjects offered to pupils?

How can we improve the range of our out-of-school activities?

In order to explain the causal links between the characteristic features, it is necessary to identify and, where appropriate and possible, to control the variables involved. A variable is a characteristic of a phenomenon that can change or be changed. It can therefore take on different values and these can be observed, and in many cases, measured.

Analytical research involves classifying data into categories that are of your own devising, rather than using a categorisation that is imposed by external factors. This helps to provide a more systematic structure than that provided by a descriptive account, and will help in clarifying the principles that underpin explanation as to why particular things are grouped together and may suggest relationships between groupings that are worthy of examination. This gives rise to three types of analytical structures.

1. Synoptic accounts where narrative is broken up into distinct blocks such as periods of history. In historical analysis, for example, the reign of Henry VIII might be broken up into various periods, and the crucial focus may be on the transition from one period to another, rather than on a mass of less significant events within each period.

2. Disaggregated accounts where complex processes are systematically broken down into a series of component parts, and each part may be explored using whatever research method, theoretical or conceptual framework and data which may be appropriate for that part. The historical processes at work in one period of Henry VIII's reign could be categorised into political, theological, economic, social, cultural and technological, and a different model of explanation could be developed for each, as well as an analytical model of how they might be inter-related.

3. Multi-causal accounts go beyond categorising different aspects of the phenomenon and attempt to show how the factors that contribute to complicated processes with multiple causes are patterned so that these causes may be weighed and balanced against each other, and considered long-term or short-term causes, and whether they are necessary but not sufficient, or sufficient in themselves. This approach can become very sophisticated to the point of producing an algorithmic model of the process under examination.

Analytical structures which

1. use simple but strong categories and
2. clearly define distinctive collections of data will provide some useful benefits in organising a thesis.

What is needed is a limited range of substantial, broad concepts. It is not helpful to get bogged down in explaining fine distinctions that are inappropriate for this kind of organising, and the ideas behind the categorisation should be readily identifiable by the reader. Over-categorisation in terms of both the chapter structure of the thesis and the contents of any given chapter carries with it the danger of the loss on the part of the reader of any sense of coherence or inter-connectedness. The writing may become opaque and the analysis over-extended. Too great an emphasis on multiple layers of categories and sub-structures of analysis is not to be recommended.

Predictive research

As the name suggests, this type of research seeks to predict from the analysis of a particular situation whether it is likely to recur elsewhere. On the basis of research already carried out it seeks to suggest whether or not a specific phenomenon is likely to appear in a similar situation. It therefore tries to address such problems as:

How would an increase or decrease in the price of our product affect the level of sales?

What kind of advertising is likely to increase sales?

In what area of the country should we open a new motor showroom in order to obtain a given level of sales?

Will the introduction of a new holiday scheme reduce staff turnover?

In this way the solution to a particular problem, which is the subject of the research, will be sought in similar studies elsewhere to see if the solution they contain is applicable in this case. A clear understanding of the possible relevant causal links is required if an appropriate solution is to be found, and such research involves estimating which variable needs to be adjusted in order to bring about the required change.

It has been suggested above that the processes involved in research may be quantitative or qualitative. Most researchers tend to have a natural orientation towards one or the other and will feel most comfortable with their preferred approach.

Quantitative Processes

Quantitative methods provided the basis of much research in the twentieth century, based on the notion that all knowledge stems from direct observation and from logical inferences derived from direct observation: an idea based on the philosophical school known as logical positivism. In natural science, this required isolating and observing phenomena and describing the patterns detected in mathematical laws, to provide an understanding of nature.

This approach has had considerable influence on the conduct of research in the social sciences, giving rise to the idea that people can be objectively studied in the same way as natural phenomena. It is indeed the case that the behaviour of people in the mass can give rise to patterns which can be detected and eventually used for predictive purposes e.g. in public opinion polls predicting voting behaviour.

The use of statistical methods in looking for relationships and patterns of behaviour and attempting to measure them with a view to expressing these numerically is often an important component in this type of research.

Two kinds of statistics are commonly employed

1. descriptive statistics and
2. inferential statistics.

1. Descriptive statistics describes patterns of behaviour and relationships between them. However, more than this, these techniques use tables, charts, graphs and other diagrams to present data. The advantage of this approach is that it may make for easier identification of patterns and relationships that may not be immediately discernible in

the raw data. As a means of conducting a preliminary exploration of the data, or as the complete analysis if full statistical rigour is not necessary, or the nature of the data does not justify it, then these techniques have much to offer. It is not merely the case of using more compact forms to present data, but using the forms to assist in detecting possible hypotheses that can then be tested using inferential statistics.

2. Inferential statistics seek to establish generalisations from samples of populations under investigation on the basis of probability. The focus here is on the study of average or group effects rather than individual differences, and is the kind of focus pursued in natural science. Inferential statements derived from this analytical model relate to groups of people or events and are based in probability theory. In experimental research, the objective is to establish aggregate differences between groups or categories of subjects. The emphasis is on

(a) precision of measurement and
(b) controlling extraneous sources of error.

The variable being studied (the independent variable) is therefore isolated and manipulated in order to observe and measure the effect of the manipulation on the second (dependent) variable. As the extraneous variables are controlled, a causal relationship between two or more variables of interest may be inferred.

Two processes are generally required to establish methodological control. Both rely on the principle of randomness.

(a) Random sampling, which requires selecting subjects from the population being studied in such a way that each member of the population has an equal chance (or known probability) of being selected. Typically, this may be done through the use of random number tables, or an appropriate computer program that generates selection on the same basis. This allows the generalisation of the results of the research from the sample to the population being studied.

(b) Randomisation allocates subjects to groups or experimental circumstances or situations in such a way that each subject has an equal chance of being selected for each circumstance or situation. The random distribution of subject characteristics in every respect other than the manipulation involved in the experiment (or treatment in the case of medicine) allows the possibility of inferring that any differences between the groups which result from the manipulation must be due to the variable which has been isolated.

While this technique has a clear relevance to the natural sciences, and may be pursued in some areas of psychology, it cannot be used so readily in the social sciences where the aspect of experimental control may be impractical or unethical. Thus, the randomisation of subjects into groups to receive or not receive treatment may not be possible or acceptable. A quasi-experimental design is therefore sometimes used in the social sciences. This maintains the basic logic of experimental research while relaxing some of the control stipulated by the experimental method. Thus, a systematic empirical approach is employed without experimental manipulation, or the assigning of subjects to circumstances or situations does not occur either because the events have already taken place or cannot be subjected to manipulation. In this way, the causal statements of the experimental method become statements of correlation in the quasi-experimental context. Correlation in itself does not necessarily indicate causality although some causal form of events may sometimes be inferred. A theoretical model is vital here as the basis of an empirical study to help in the interpretation of the results of the research.

The final form of the dissertation will be affected by the research strategy adopted. Commonly, research strategy in social science may involve comparison between two groups. This involves the allocation of subjects to independent but equivalent groups that are used for each experimental or control condition. The control group here offers a benchmark for comparison. Both the experimental and groups are given pre-tests and post-tests, but the treatment or intervention is given only to the experimental group. The impact of the intervention can then be evaluated by comparing the results for the experimental group with those for the control group.

This research design enables the impact of experimental interventions to be attributed to the interventions themselves rather than some extraneous variable. It is absolutely necessary, however, for the subjects to have been assigned to the groups by some means that is genuinely random. Where randomisation is not possible, it becomes necessary to demonstrate that the two groups are equivalent even though not derived from the identical population of subjects. This equivalence is demonstrated by matching the two groups on the variables that are vital to the realisation of the research, whether these are age, gender, race, social class or some other characteristic.

Another potential problem with this basic design is that the pre-test evaluation may itself have some influence on the subjects, and the design does not control for this. It may arise because in some kinds of pre-test evaluation can alert subjects to the fact that they are now taking part in a study or might provide some degree of practice which may influence the results of the post-test and hence the validity of the outcomes.

It may be that a post-test only can eliminate this problem, but the point here is that problems do not end when the research design has been chosen, and there will remain issues surrounding possible sources of error and the existence of competing explanations that can account for a set of results.

Experimental research designs are mostly variations on this format based on treatment or intervention and control. Their popularity rests on their ability to allow causal inferences to be made about the variable and their relationships. The data, which are generated by using an experimental intervention, are evaluated by the application of statistical techniques that measure the differences within and between groups. These techniques include the analysis of variance or a t-test, measuring the extent of differences within groups arising from variability between individuals against the extent of differences between groups.

By contrast, correlational designs are based on comparing the distribution of scores dispersed along two dimensions e.g. the incidence of lung cancer and cigarette smoking. Inferential statistics are also used in these studies, but the techniques involved are those of regression analysis and significance testing and are much used in research that depends on questionnaire surveys, scales etc to generalise findings from samples to populations of interest.

It is important to remember, however, that the kind of statements that can be made about relationships between variables is determined by the research design, NOT the statistical method employed.

It must also be noted that however appropriate and sophisticated the statistical techniques employed, they cannot compensate for an inappropriate research design.

You must remember that:

- the same data can often be analysed in different ways and
- both the experimental and correlational approaches may be equally valid.

Two further points relating to quantitative research.

(i) Do not place undue emphasis on establishing findings that are statistically significant. They may not be significant in any practical sense. The real importance is whether the findings are significant in a social, scientific or clinical sense.

The objective is to make important inferences about some form of behaviour NOT to achieve results that are statistically significant. Correlation coefficients may, for example, suggest the degree of relationship between two variables and thus be more useful than establishing the existence or otherwise of statistical significance. In this way the use of diagrammatic illustrations of data including graphs, scatter diagrams, pie and bar charts etc may be more instructive than any amount of sophisticated statistical computation.

(ii) You need to understand and ACCEPT that good research is the result of a compromise between

  (a) eliminating the influence of as many variables as possible which might confuse the issue and

  (b) failing to use any controls in fieldwork observations.

In (a) your results may be stated with complete confidence but prove to be totally uninteresting. In (b) your results may be fascinating but unreliable and impossible to replicate. There has been a constant shifting of emphasis in leaning towards one pole and then to the other. Currently, the pendulum seems to have swung towards seeking the greatest degree of meaning possible and the number and scope of acceptable research strategies with which to pursue this has correspondingly expanded. Nevertheless, there are still many areas of research, particularly in clinical and scientific areas, where the emphasis is still placed on control in an experimental research design. In these experimental and quasi-experimental designs, the research

 (i) controls as much of the study as possible;

 (ii) focuses on a restricted area of behaviour – sometimes a single variable;

(iii) is carried out by a researcher who seeks to be objective and detached.

One criticism that is often levied at experimental studies is that they can sometimes tend to be narrow and artificial. To counter this tendency some researchers, particularly in areas of the social sciences, have developed research techniques aimed at being both flexible and spontaneous. These relatively new techniques have presented an epistemological and philosophical challenge to the established research tradition in both science and social science. Some supporters of the new approaches have challenged the applicability of science based on logical positivism to studies of individual and social human behaviour and have questioned the whole concept of the objective, neutral observer. It is argued that the very presence of an observer influences whatever is being observed. The investigator and the investigated cannot be separated.

Criticism has also come from other quarters on other grounds. For example, feminists criticise the experimental method as traditionally utilised on the grounds that it commonly involves a (usually) male researcher dominating some kind of power hierarchy, although whether an experimental or non-experimental method is used tells you nothing about the researcher's (of either gender) approach to non-sexist investigation.

The use of the term 'qualitative' covers a whole range of approaches, and what they have in common is usually the collection of data in the form of words rather than numbers. Descriptive and inferential statistics are replaced by themes, categories and subjective evaluation. There is less emphasis on the testing of an hypothesis and much more on discovery and description. The categories generated from qualitative data are of particular utility in understanding human behaviour and assist the understanding of the meaning people give to the events they experience and interpret.

Qualitative methods provide rich, in-depth data as opposed to the manipulation and recording of previously identified variables typical of quantitative research, and would be supported by its practitioners on the grounds that experimental and non-experimental methods cannot appropriately and sensitively describe many aspects of human experience e.g. the emotional trauma of undergoing a major surgical operation. This is not to say that qualitative research employs a unique and distinct set of methods. It may use interviews, surveys, participant and non-participant observation or the interpretation of texts that is hermeneutics. A specialist in ethnographic research, for example, might employ interviews and observations. In general terms, however, it may be suggested that quantitative research involves measures of frequency, quantity or intensity, whereas qualitative research emphasises process and meaning.

This implies for many qualitative researchers

(i) reality is a social construct;
(ii) there is a close relationship between what is studied and the researcher;
(iii) the investigation is influenced by its context.

In spite of the diversity of research methods that may be described as qualitative, they all tend to be underpinned by a common basis of understanding.

(i) An holistic approach – the whole is more than the sum of the parts. In order, therefore, to comprehensively understand the subject of the research, the research method used has to enable the researcher to understand the complete and entire phenomenon, whereas experimental methods isolate and measure variables with narrow definition, and understanding is obtained through control and prediction.

(ii) Inductive reasoning beginning from particular observations that lead to the identification of a general pattern from the cases that have been identified. No assumptions are made about possible relationships between the data before observations are made in contrast to the approach of experimental designs using hypotheses and deductive reasoning that requires hypotheses and variables to be specified before data is collected.

(iii) Data is collected in its naturally occurring state, as the purpose is to discover and understand phenomena in its natural context. This is, again, in contrast to experimental research with its use of controls and a narrow range of variables and therefore outcomes.

Exactly which qualitative method may be appropriately selected is a matter of context and also often the particular discipline involved and its research tradition. Disciplines such as anthropology and sociology have a long tradition of using ethnography as a qualitative method.

The field of qualitative methods is very complex today and any attempt at a classification of these methods runs the risk of over-simplification. However, one classification that is commonly used is that of

  (i) phenomenology
 (ii) hermeneutics
(iii) ethnography.

These research traditions are distinguished principally by

(a) their view of the nature of knowledge;
(b) the problems which concern the researcher;
(c) how the researcher relates to the subject matter.

These dimensions are relative to the identified qualitative research traditions in the following ways.

Their view of the nature of knowledge

Phenomenology is focused on what is the nature of experience, consciousness, rather than what causes the experience.

Hermeneutics engages in dialogue with a text, constantly returning to it in order to increase understanding and to establish an increasingly comprehensive interpretation.

Ethnography may use description and interpretation (inductive reasoning) or work from theory (deductive reasoning).

The concerns of the researcher

Phenomenology – the researcher seeks to describe the experience of the individual independently of any theoretical or social constraints, and attempts to understand the significance of human phenomena as the individual experiences it.

Hermeneutics – the researcher seeks to obtain an in-depth understanding of the setting of the text and its meaning as derived from the context.

Ethnography – the researcher seeks to understand how groups, organisations, communities or societies make sense of the experience of their lives, world, group or society so that this can be explored, interpreted and explained.

How the researcher relates to the subject matter

Phenomenology – interviewing commonly enables the researcher to play a role in constructing the narrative.

Hermeneutics – the involvement of the researcher in explaining the text is very intensive, and this enters into the data context.

Ethnography – the researcher makes no assumptions, remains as detached as possible, but is also totally involved with the subject matter.

Phenomenology

This tradition focuses on the experience of the individual, and attempts to convey this in a way that reflects that experience as accurately as possible. It involves, therefore, an attempt not only to describe but also to elucidate the meaning of people's experience, to a greater extent than any other research method. Beyond how people's experiences are described, phenomenology attempts to explore the underlying structure of consciousness in order to arrive at the essential nature of ideas. Interviewing is typically used to collect data, often in the form of extended conversations, so the skills involved are listening (more difficult than many people think!), empathizing with the interviewee and observing e.g. the body language during the interview. The researcher notes any themes that become apparent during the discussion, but does not at this stage attempt to analyse or give any structure or meaning to the observations. After the observations have been duly noted, analysis may take place which may involve reducing and reconstructing the data.

Two approaches may be identified in phenomenological research.

(a) The 'empirical' approach is where the researcher uses open-ended questions and conversation with the subject and then collects their personal descriptions of a particular experience. The structural nature of the experience is then described by reflecting upon and interpreting the participant's account in an analytical way. Among the writers associated with this approach are van Kaam (1966) and Giorgi (1985).

(b) The 'heuristic' approach whereby the researcher seeks to explore a research question that is socially significant as well as having personal meaning for the researcher in terms of illuminating the relationship between the self and the social world. Moustakas (1994) studied loneliness in this context and distinguished the heuristic approach from the empirical approach in two ways.

   (i) It maintains a closer relationship with the narratives of individuals during the research process.
   (ii) The sources of data are wider than descriptive accounts offered by participants and may include personal journals, diaries, artwork, and fictional stories provided by the participants and go beyond considering one particular aspect or situation in the participant's life.

Hermeneutics

This approach is used to provide an enhanced comprehension of the context in which data are found and which gives it meaning. It involves the interpretation of text or transcribed meanings, and as such was pioneered by scholars using textual analysis in seeking to establish the meaning of obscure texts in the Christian Bible. Subsequently, this was adopted for the study of secular texts by social scientists.

Two contrasting positions are found in the hermeneutics approach.

(i) The text has meaning quite separately and independently of the researcher – the 'objective' approach.

(ii) All understanding is basically derived from the active involvement of the interpreter with the data – the 'constructive' approach. Understanding is thus derived from fusing together the different perspectives of the interpreter and the data or event. The argument here is that we all have our own perspectives drawn from our life experiences and our expectations based on these experiences but these are inevitably limited as is our expression of them, so that interaction between the text and the reader assists us to bring about a greater degree of comprehension.

One difficulty with this latter approach is that the analysis of texts in their historical, social or cultural context may be undertaken in order to apply their significant lessons to contemporary questions. This requires both the comprehension of the meaning of the data in a way that makes it intelligible to the contemporary audience and the capacity to remain true to the original context of the data. This is a very difficult task to resolve satisfactorily, but can give rise to the establishment of some interesting research questions.

The difference between hermeneutics and phenomenology should be clear. In the former, the researcher is provided with the data and the research task is to make sense of it using hermeneutic techniques, whereas in the latter the researcher is involved in creating the data via interviews and transcription of the recorded conversation or narrative.

Hermeneutics involves a difficult and often complex research process. It requires

(i) constant recourse to the data source;
(ii) establishing a dialogue with this data;
(iii) seeking to establish what the data meant to its source or creator;
(iv) fusing together the meaning derived from (iii) with the meaning placed upon it by the researcher.

Given that research in the Social Sciences frequently involves the researcher in seeking to understand the contexts of phenomena, notions and emotions, in this sense hermeneutics is necessarily entailed in a great deal of research. However, as a formal research method it is relatively unusual and tends not to receive much coverage in many books on research methods although there are specialist works such as Taylor (1990). The best-known examples of the application of the technique may be found in the work of Jung (1938) and Packer (1985).

Packer successfully extended the use of the hermeneutic approach to the study of any kind of human activity arguing that every action has its context that can be regarded as 'textual' in its structure. Whereas empirical or rationalist orientations provide you with a map or plan of a location, hermeneutics is a description provided by someone who actually inhabits the location, lives its daily life, and knows the geography from daily personal experience of living there. It is the difference between an abstraction that is formally produced and a perspective that may be partial and prejudiced but is also intensely individual.

The hermeneutics approach may involve the study of a wide range of materials relating to the subject of the research including newspapers and press releases, other media, reports from conferences and workshops, academic and other papers and reports, whether formal or informal, and audio and videotapes. Some of this material may be obtained from the Internet.

Ethnography

This paradigm derives from anthropology and focuses on some particular aspects of the life of a specific group in terms of behaviour, habits, practices and usages in relation to these particular aspects. Essentially, it focuses on the informants' accounts and detailed descriptions.

There is a range of ethnographic inquiry that can be utilised from the inductive development of theory out of the process of description and interpretation to the deductive use of existing theoretical frameworks to construct the research. The difficult task in the ethnographic approach is to combine the establishment and management of total involvement (immersion) in the chosen setting while maintaining the necessary level of detachment from the focus of the research. This approach has traditionally been employed by anthropologists such as Mead (1928) and Malinowski (1922; 1926). Another groundbreaking study in this paradigm was that of Goffman (1961) in a mental health setting.

The research data may consist of fieldwork using observations and interactions, follow-up qualitative interviews recorded verbatim as well as notes on archival research and artifacts. The data thus derived are clearly likely to be copious and difficult to handle and is therefore reduced by the use of the constant comparative method. This involves the following process:

(i) systematic coding of the data into themes and categories;
(ii) identification and refinement of the emerging categories;
(iii) relating the categories together in some logical way;
(iv) consideration of the theoretical implications of the nature of the category relationships;
(v) establishing a pattern from the theoretical properties of the categories.

The term 'grounded theory' is applied to the pattern that is identified following Glaser and Strauss (1967). This is because the theory is grounded in the data and is not derived externally.

The adoption of a qualitative approach to research has implications for the way in which a research proposal and study may be written.

1. These approaches are not commonly used to test hypotheses.
2. The theoretical frameworks may evolve with the progress of the research and the analysis of data.
3. A provisional conceptual framework will provide a focus to the study and place boundaries around it.
4. The literature review will provide the ideas about the events, settings, processes and theoretical constructs which the researcher will bring to the study.

Thus, a qualitative study might involve a government decision to reorganise the National Health Service (event) in Scotland (setting), interactions between interested groups, government departments and Parliament (processes), and decision-making in governmental settings (theoretical frameworks).

5. The purpose of the research question or questions is to focus the researcher on the objective of the study including explaining the theoretical bases and approach.
6. The research question will suggest the range of research methods that it might be possible to usefully employ.
7. The research question may be adjusted as the research progresses and brings to light more information and perspectives.
8. It is essential for the researcher to be aware of his/her own perspectives, assumptions, values and expectations for the research. No-one comes to research in a totally objective way and it is critical that the researcher makes clear his/her position on relevant issues while seeking to maintain the rigour of the research with no pre-determined programme or agenda of their own.

9. The research methods will need to include built-in safeguards to reduce as far as possible the danger of the researcher influencing the data.

10. The prevalence of detailed description and direct quotations from participants will influence the way results are presented.

It is important that no prospective researcher should assume that qualitative research is in some sense easier than quantitative approaches. The testing of hypotheses by the use of appropriate statistical tests is replaced by the awesome problem of handling copious amounts of intractable data from interview transcripts and similar material to provide a logical arrangement to assist understanding – an enormous task. Whatever approach is taken and whatever paradigm adopted, the hard work of research – the up-front thinking to determine a precise and focused research question or hypothesis remains the significant hurdle to be overcome.

At this point you might well raise the question of why a thesis necessarily has to follow either a quantitative or a qualitative approach. Surely there is scope in some cases for using both approaches in the same thesis? There are indeed benefits that can be derived from using both paradigms in some combination. There are, however, also dangers which have to be recognised and which are very real to the extent that some authors e.g. Moccia (1988) argue strongly against any such combination. The major danger involved is that the two types of data may be conflated together to support an argument in ways that are inappropriate. For example, it may be that the quantitative side of the research does not support an hypothesis in the way a researcher hoped and it is easy therefore to downplay this and to bring in and emphasise qualitative data, perhaps even giving them a numerical perspective, in order to arrive at the desired answer. This is, of course, unacceptable. However, while it may seem obvious, as clearly the two types of data need to be used for different purposes, it is nevertheless a trap into which it is easy to almost unwittingly fall.

The objections of other authors stem from an overwhelming commitment to one or other paradigm that they regard as involving assumptions that are not compatible with theirs. This may be due in some cases, of course, to the nature and uses of the other paradigm. In epistemological terms, quantitative studies are seen as employing the 'objectivist' approach, which validates knowledge by proposing theories as potentially universally applicable hypotheses, which are then subjected to empirical tests. Qualitative studies by contrast, are orientated towards the 'constructivist' approach where knowledge is validated through internal consistency and social constructs, and where the theory may be derived from the data. Knowledge is seen here as being located within specific contexts and cannot be validated on the basis of one reality from which deductive processes may be used for the purpose of validating theories.

The purpose of using two approaches in combination is largely to try to obtain the scientific rigour of quantitative designs and data while also benefiting from the greater degree of understanding that qualitative design and data may provide. There are a number of ways in which designs may combine the two models – sequentially; simultaneously in parallel; equal status where each approach is used to aid understanding equally in their own way; and the dominant approach where one is used to supplement in a relatively small way the major paradigm (Cresswell, 1995).

Another approach favoured by Tashakkori and Teddie (1998) is to combine aspects of both methodologies in the course of the investigation quite pragmatically. They regard the question of research methods as being subordinate to the adoption of a paradigm that guides the research in an over-riding fashion. This approach allows the adoption of both hypotheses to be tested empirically alongside questions which need to be explored in a more general way, and thus uses both quantitative data collection techniques e.g. questionnaires, alongside interview and observational approaches, with quantitative analytical procedures being applied to the questionnaire data with qualitative analysis of themes and categories derived from the interview and observational data.

An approach commonly suggested by students is to undertake a large-scale questionnaire survey, perhaps using rating scales or similar closed questions, and then to use interviews with a random sample from the original sample to discuss interesting points that have arisen from the analysis of the questionnaire. This assumes that current research knowledge of the area permits the construction of an adequate questionnaire and that the interview sample would be in a position to discuss the points of interest. A sufficiently large random sample from the original group might allow for this but a sufficiently large initial and secondary group is pre-supposed – something that is not always available. If the questionnaire is treated as being anonymous or confidential then it is not, of course, possible to select and interview those respondents who may have had something interesting to say e.g. in response to an open-ended question in the questionnaire.

Ultimately, the opportunities for combining the two paradigms may be relatively limited, with the possible exception of case studies. While, on the one hand, it may be argued that statistical approaches merely provide complex information in a convenient way and that qualitative data provides possibly more complex information in a way that is less convenient because its complexity does not allow it to be reduced in the same way, it should also be remembered that often what is possible may depend on the existing state of knowledge. Where knowledge is totally or almost lacking, the use of a questionnaire too soon in the knowledge acquisition process may prejudice subsequent investigation and knowledge. This is where the exploration process has an effective contribution to make as a thesis, and may be followed by other theses that test the hypotheses derived from the initial exploratory process and this might involve questionnaire techniques for example. This could be followed by the application of the theories to case studies as a means of either confirming that they do stand up to the rigours of application to individual situations or that they are in need of amendment or further development. The state of knowledge about any particular phenomenon should be reflected in the research question or questions formulated, and this will indicate the likely range of effective research methods. It may well be that practicalities will then determine which methods are actually applied.

Case studies themselves constitute an approach that may use both qualitative and quantitative techniques. This approach is both widely used and almost as widely abused. All too often a case study lacks structure and consists of a series of descriptions of haphazardly chosen features or aspects in an unrelated way. In this manner, data may be thrown 'like mud' at a series of targets in an uncoordinated way. An appropriately structured framework is as essential to case studies as to any other research approach. Other dangers include the temptation to formulate generalizations or theories on the basis of the slight evidence that may emerge from a unique case, while it is frequently the case that the researcher has some association with the case, which may give rise to subjectivity in relation to the issues of interpretation and selection of data.

The case study is essentially a detailed account of a particular example of a phenomenon, experience, event or situation. Its purpose is not to demonstrate causal relationships or to test hypotheses, although case studies may contribute to theory building (Gill and Johnson, 1997). In the case study, context is of central importance and it is necessary for clearly defined boundaries to be placed around the area for study. Examples of boundaries within which case studies might be applied include patients with a particular medical problem e.g. cystic fibrosis; students on a three-year course of teacher training; a particular college or one of its departments; a factory, office, company, or trade union branch; or the process whereby a government arrived at a particular policy decision e.g. to re-organise the

National Health Service in England. These instances would all be referred to as units of analysis. This is the unit about which detailed information is required. Any researcher who is contemplating a case study should consult the work of Yin (1981; 1994), Stake (1995) and Hamel et al. (1994).

Case studies may be appropriate in a number of situations, as Scapins (1990) has suggested.

1. Where the objective is restricted to describing current practice.
2. Where it is intended to illustrate new and potentially innovative practices that have been adopted by a particular organisation or organisations.
3. Where the research examines the difficulties in implementing new procedures and techniques in an organisation and in evaluating their benefits.
4. Where existing theory is used to understand and explain what is happening.
5. Where there is insufficient knowledge to enable hypotheses to be established and/or where there is a lack of theorization.

Sometimes, as Otley and Berry (1994) point out, it also happens that chance circumstances throw an opportunity in the way of a researcher such that access is permitted which allows the examination of a phenomenon. Even if it is not possible in these circumstances to examine all the aspects of the particular case that might be relevant, the results can still be worthwhile.

In some instance, of course, case studies may combine elements of two or more of the above types.

Yin (1994) has suggested that case study research displays the following characteristics.

1. The research aims not only to explore certain phenomena, but to understand them within a certain context.
2. The research does not commence with a set of questions and notions about the limits within which the study will take place.

3. The research uses multiple methods for collecting data that may be both qualitative and quantitative.

Case studies tend towards phenomenological approaches, but there is no reason why a more positivistic approach should not be taken if appropriate, with a stronger role for theoretical frameworks and the investigation of specific research questions within the case study structure.

Hussey and Hussey (1997) have identified a number of stages in the research process that apply to case studies whatever the paradigmatic emphasis given to the particular project.

1. Select the case. This may often be a matter of practicality but a number of points may be borne in mind.

   (a) A representative case or set of cases is not commonly necessary (or indeed may not be available) as statistical generalizations from a sample to a larger population are not involved.

   (b) A theory that has been proposed from one set of circumstances may be applied to the particular set of circumstances of the given case study to test whether the generalizations hold good in this case.

   (c) A case may be selected to include the issues that are of most importance to you.

   (d) A series of similar cases may suggest whether a theory can be generalised – dissimilar cases may suggest the need to amend the theory in some way.

2. Initial preliminary investigation

   Become familiar with the context of your research.
   Reflect on the paradigm you have chosen.
   Examine what you consider to be the purpose of your research.
   Determine whether you feel you wish to try and rid your mind of any prior bias and to learn from the evidence that presents itself at this stage or whether you consider you are approaching the study with explicit or implicit theories.

3. The data stage

   (i) Determine the qualitative and quantitative data you will collect.

   (ii) Determine data collection methods e.g. online searching, interviews, questionnaires, and observation.

   (iii) Determine how, where, and when to collect data.

4. The analysis stage

   (i) Determine whether to use:

      (a) within-case analysis or
      (b) cross-case analysis.

   (ii) If using within-case analysis:

      (a) familiarise yourself totally with the material
      (b) build up separate descriptions of events, opinions, phenomena in order to identify patterns.

   (iii) If using cross-case analysis:

      (a) identify similarities and differences
      (b) use these to identify common patterns.

5 The report stage

   (i) Determine an appropriate structure e.g. chronological.

   (ii) Link the analysis and conclusions to the mass of data collected.

      (a) Quote extensively from the data collected from interviews and other sources, particularly in a phenomenological study.

      (b) Use diagrams wherever possible to illustrate and explain the emerging patterns.

There are sometimes problems and weaknesses associated with case studies.

1. Access to an appropriate organisation can be difficult.

2. It is a very time-consuming research approach in terms of process.

3. It is sometimes difficult to determine the boundaries of the study – an organisation or group of individuals interact

with the rest of society. The nature of these interactions between the sample being studied and the rest of society inevitably occur between the sample and other organisations, groups or individuals. This can change the group dynamics of the study and the attitudes of those within the group being studied.

4. It is often necessary to be aware of the history of your unit of analysis and also its likely future as these may influence understanding of the present.

Another question that by now will have occurred to some readers is whether it is necessary to concern oneself with the problem of collecting data at all. Why not write a thesis that concerns itself solely with theory – perhaps a work of advanced criticism such as that written by Peter Self (1972). Before even contemplating such an option it would be wise to read one or two such works in order to get some idea of the immense intellectual task that is involved. It represents a formidable challenge and may require intellectual attributes of an unusual order. It certainly involves total familiarity with the literature in the particular field and with its areas of debate and controversy in order to generate new theory. This is not to say that theoretical implications may not arise from a more usual empirical study and ultimately result in new or revised theorization, but this is something that emerges incidentally from the study rather than being its prime purpose.

Essentially, a theoretically focused thesis has to present an argument based on the literature that suggests that there is a significant new way in which some particular phenomenon can be comprehended. One viable way of approaching such a thesis is to draw upon two or more quite distinct fields and integrate them in such a way as to provide a fresh understanding e.g. by constructing a model which shows newly established inter-relationships using key components from the cited fields. The model may, of course, be subsequently subjected to empirical testing.

Another approach to thesis writing uses what is called Meta-Analysis. This uses existing data from different studies on the same subject to produce a secondary form of analysis by comparing and pooling the results. The argument in favour of such analyses is that by utilizing as many studies as possible the researcher is provided with a depth of comprehension of the subject of study, which is beyond the bounds of any single study.

Glass (1976) described meta-analysis as an "analysis of analyses". Certain steps are involved.

1. Relevant studies are examined for the rigour of their research methods.
2. Those whose rigour is considered acceptable are used for the analysis.
3. The data or findings from all these studies are reduced to a common basis using appropriate statistical techniques.
4. The larger new sample is used to explore relationships among the variables.

Essentially, in this form of analysis, it is the literature review together with a careful statistical analysis that provides the research base for the thesis. Clearly, however, it is necessary to have an adequate number of previously conducted and acceptable studies before the use of this technique can even be considered.

Action research may provide another basis for a thesis while presenting formidable problems to the researcher. Its principal purpose is to generate knowledge in order to advance social change and analysis. Greenwood and Levin (1998:6) provide some precise definitions. In this way it is quite different from the kind of theory-based research carried out for academic purposes.

Action research may use a wide diversity of techniques, both quantitative and qualitative, and including inter alia, surveys, interviews, focus groups, and statistical techniques. The purpose and objectives of the research may well be determined by the members of the group concerned themselves engaging in some form of participation and problem identification. In this way, the members of the group at the heart of the problem become partners in the research, while the researcher fills the role of facilitator whose skills need to be based in, and predominantly used, to encourage the group to focus on their own behaviour patterns such as resistance to change. The theoretical aspect of the research is represented by the necessity to understand the context or framework within which the problem to be tackled is situated. This is clearly a somewhat different undertaking from the more conventional approaches to formulating and writing a thesis, and presents difficulties in translating the work into an academic context.

The concept of action research was developed further by Argyris et al. (1985) in the form of 'action science', which involves solving the immediate problem while developing scientific knowledge and an underpinning theory.

The following stages are typically involved in action research (HOD, 1998).

1. Identify a problem area.
2. Form hypotheses or predictions that imply a goal and a procedure for achieving it.
3. Carefully record the actions taken and desired goal.
4. Form inferences based on the data relating to the actions taken to the intent of achieving the desired goal.
5. Continue retesting the generalizations in the situation in an ongoing iterative process.

Susman and Evered (1978) have suggested an action research cycle:

1. analysis
2. action planning
3. implementation
4. evaluation
5. learning.

The particular importance of the learning phase is that new issues and problems are identified here, leading to a new cycle of research in what becomes a continuous learning process.

Overall, the position today in relation to research methods seems to be that the positivist approach, which maintains that the method of the natural sciences is universally applicable, would no longer be regarded as acceptable. Nevertheless, the emphasis of positivism on scientific rigour and empirical observation remains a central theme in social science research. Meanwhile, the debate as to which paradigm may ultimately prove the most valuable remains unresolved and quite probably never will be. What is essential is that you set out on your research project by defining clearly the important question to which you seek an answer, and then establish which research method will provide such an answer with both conceptual and methodological validity. To do so you will need to approach any research method with flexibility and clarity of understanding in terms of its strengths and weaknesses or limitations and its implications for assumptions about the research subject.

This, therefore, brings us naturally to the topic of over-riding importance and the subject of the next chapter – how to establish a clear and focused research question.

Tutorial

Progress questions

1. Determine the essential characteristics of research that are likely to prove acceptable to the university
2. For what research purposes would you use quantitative and qualitative techniques respectively?
3. What benefits might be derived from using quantitative and qualitative techniques together in the same research project? What might be the attendant dangers?
4. What do you understand by the case study approach? What are its advantages and disadvantages?

Discussion points

1. With which research paradigm do you feel most comfortable? Why do you think this is so?
2. What do you consider to be the attributes of a successful research project?

Practical assignment

Choose two or three research projects that you might be interested in undertaking. Consider carefully the research paradigm that might be appropriate for each. Justify your choice of paradigm and indicate what you think the limitations might be in each case.

Study tips
Write down on index cards the subject(s), field(s) or topic(s) where you might be interested in conducting research and make a note of the possible research paradigms and types of research that might be appropriate for each, listing the advantages and disadvantages of these in the context of each subject, field or topic.

3 The Research Question

One-minute overview

The doctoral researcher needs to establish a clear, precise research question that is neither too narrow nor too broad. The choice of research question has a significant impact upon the research method adopted. A topic may be derived from previous work you have done, from journal articles, conference papers, brainstorming, or the use of analogy, relevance trees or morphological analysis. An alternative approach is to try a sentence-completion technique to force clarity of thought.

It is fair to say that by far the most common problem that arises with PhD theses, particularly in the social sciences and related fields, is that the research question lacks a clear focus. It may be inadequately or ambiguously defined, or it may have been couched in terms that are too broad or too vague. The consequence of this is that it never becomes clear exactly what the research is about and this inevitably has negative effects upon the choice of research methods and mode of analysis and on the structure of the thesis that may leave central questions concerning the research unanswered. As an outcome, the discussion at the viva stage may be fraught with difficulty and the thesis failed or returned for major amendments.

The first thing to do is to pick a topic – which can be astonishingly difficult. There is often a tendency to go for something that is either much too big or much too small or even trivial. Usually the tendency is initially to choose something which is too big if only because the prospect of having to write 75,000 words or whatever the usual length of the PhD is in your institution suggests that something extensive is called for in order to get near the maximum word limit (which is erroneously what is thought to be required). When this is found to be overwhelming and difficult to make sense of, there may be a tendency to veer to the opposite extreme where the danger is that a trivial topic will yield neither sufficient research sources nor sufficient interest to sustain effort during the difficult times to come.

It is essential to pick a subject in which you have a genuine interest as you will be working on it for a long time and will suffer sufficient frustration, boredom and loss of interest during this time without having to endure a subject which has absolutely no interest for you at all. This is an obvious recipe for failure.

Unless you are fortunate enough to be a member of a research team covering a particular area of research e.g. technical education, where you may be handed a specific topic to research e.g. the role of the technical school in England and Wales, 1944–1965, then the problem of choosing a topic is likely to fall to you to resolve largely unaided.

There are no rules of thumb that can be offered for choosing a topic. You may start from something about which you already know a great deal or in which you have a real interest – perhaps something about which you wrote a tutorial or seminar paper in an undergraduate or master's course and which might be worth developing. Most people probably come to doctoral research with an idea of what they wish to do – what is needed is the refinement of the topic into a viable, manageable and useful research question. A word of caution may be timely here. While it is important – even essential – to come to your research topic with interest and enthusiasm, a too close personal involvement, particularly if this leads to a strong wish for a desired outcome to support an issue close to your heart or which may advance a cause in which you are interested, may lead to a research process or analysis which is flawed or interpreted in the desired way rather than the appropriate way. You must be prepared to accept research symmetry i.e. whatever outcome emerges, and to accept negative or positive outcomes as being potentially equally important. You must also be prepared to accept that your treasured hypothesis may be rejected or that your research question is not answered in the way you had expected or hoped. This is a danger inherent in the research process – and may actually give rise to even more important and interesting questions than the original once you have accepted and examined the outcome. Another alternative is to use the journals in the library as a source to provide you with inspiration. Articles in learned journals often leave important questions unanswered because they are not the prime focus of the paper, or will suggest, directly or indirectly, areas for further research arising from the discussion. Attending conferences and listening to the papers presented may perform the same function. Having identified a field that might be of interest, it is worth checking through the Index to Theses for perhaps the last ten years or so, or any available lists of research currently going on in order to see what has already been done and what remains to be done. Useful spin-offs from which to generate ideas can be found from these sources. Bear in mind, however, that where gaps exist, they sometimes exist for good reason. It may be that the gap is too trivial to be worth the time and resources to fill – it is simply not important enough, or that although not the subject of formal research, people working in the field already have a good idea of the situation. It may be that access could not be obtained to the necessary data – do not assume that because you see a research project as being exciting and important that others are necessarily going to see it in that light as they may have reason for not wanting the research to be done. However, the fact that one researcher has been denied access does not necessarily mean that another would not be successful – access may be denied for a variety of reasons and particularly over time, the reason or reasons may disappear or it may be a matter of personalities.

Once you have determined your topic area, the next step is to narrow it down to a suitably focused research question or hypothesis. Unfortunately there is no certain way of doing this, although inevitably some degree of trial and error is involved. You may pursue various trains of thought and see where they lead you. You may conduct brainstorming sessions with yourself or with others, perhaps fellow-students in a similar position who are likely to be supportive in doing this in the expectation that you will reciprocate the favour. You may use the 'spider' technique, positioning the various possibilities at the end of each leg drawn from the body of a spider that represents the topic area. Some people simply list as many possibilities as they can think of in a personal brainstorming session. The kind of narrowing involved is demonstrated below.

As the process continues so it may become increasingly difficult as greater precision becomes necessary, and the honing down becomes increasingly focused. Thus, you may have started with a general field such as Social Policy. You may have narrowed this down to health care, and more specifically,

Topic Area	Leading to	Leading to
The organisation of the National Health Service in the United Kingdom	The organisation of the National Health Service in Scotland	The reorganisation of the National Health Service in Scotland, 1974
Women in management	Women in management in the National Health Service	The nature of support given to the development of women managers Health Service in England
Apprenticeship	Engineering apprentices	The drop-out rate of engineering apprentices from day release courses at Colleges

the organisation of the National Health Service. You may then discover that the National Health Service is organised differently in the four countries of the United Kingdom, so you may decide to focus on Scotland – perhaps because you live there or you detect that the organisation of the National Health Service there has some distinctive features of interest. You may decide you wish to explore how these features came about and look to the last time the National Health Service in Scotland was reorganised to provide some answers. Thus, your research question may become 'Why does the organisation of the National Health Service in Scotland have these features which are different from the rest of the United Kingdom?' This may involve a number of subsidiary questions e.g.

Why was the National Health Service in Scotland reorganised in this way in year X?

Why was the National Health Service in Scotland reorganised at all?

Who made the decision to proceed with reorganisation and who else was involved in it?

Who sought to influence the decision, in what ways and with what effects?

What was the relationship of the reorganisation to what (if anything) was taking place on this elsewhere in the United Kingdom?

Was the reorganisation informed by any theorisation or conceptualisation that may have framed thinking on the subject?

The important thing about subsidiary questions of this kind is that they should support the answering of the main research question, and interesting as they may prove to be in their own right, they are not the focus of the thesis and should not be allowed to become diversionary issues. They are there to help towards the answer, not to take over.

Various authors have suggested techniques for producing and refining ideas for research questions. The purpose of all these different approaches is to assist you in being specific in how you establish what your research is about – to produce the clear research question that is to be the basis of your study and to suggest possible research methods in the process.

One of the most popular techniques is 'brainstorming', which is discussed by Burnard and Morrison (1994). The benefits of brainstorming include being able to use the technique either by yourself or with a small group of your fellow students, colleagues or even friends who are willing to help – often in return for reciprocal assistance! The emphasis here is on a small group – six or eight at most is quite enough as a larger group becomes unmanageable. It is also a technique that can assist you at various stages of your research.

In order to undertake this technique you simply need

(c) ample time
(d) a supply of paper and pens
(e) to make notes as you go along (you will never remember everything afterwards).

There are various stages in the process.

1. Write down the broad general area in which you are interested e.g. business management.
2. Write down everything that occurs to you about this term, in whatever order it comes. Do not omit anything. (If you are operating in a group this task may be undertaken by a scribe who writes down all the words offered by those taking part).
3. Do this until you have either filled the page in front of you (or the scribe) or you can think of nothing else to say or write, however long the process takes – five minutes or five hours!

4. Delete any words or phrases whose immediate relevance seems doubtful – but on reflecting on some of these 'doubtful' words or phrases you may find that some do, in fact, offer striking new ideas, relationships and angles relating to the topic. One aspect of this may involve establishing links between ideas that had been unconnected at the previous stage.

5. Structure your ideas by prioritising them. This may involve developing

   (c) systematic headings and sub-headings or
   (d) a clustering of related thoughts.

6. Regularly revisit the list – throw nothing away so that you can reflect further and see how your thoughts have developed.

7. If an interesting research idea has evolved, you will need to hone it down to the clear, specific research question required; this will then move you to the stage of writing your research proposal.

If no interesting ideas emerge from the first attempt, the process can always be repeated, perhaps with a different group of participants.

Here is an example of how the process might work using the general area of business management mentioned above. The possibilities raised might include the following.

- Absenteeism from work
- The management of absenteeism
- Absenteeism as a health and safety issue
- Legal obligations of employers towards occupational health
- Involving employees in occupational health issues
- A strategic approach to occupational health
- Absence management as a team effort
- Access to occupational health services and expertise
- Problems of small businesses in relation to occupational health issues

It can be seen that simply by compiling an ad hoc list of this nature in this way questions have begun to form, and towards the end of the list the focus is becoming narrower. You will preferably need a clear research question that can be formulated in one sentence, and you may need to engage in further brainstorming to arrive at such a sentence and question.

Here are some examples of possible questions derived from the previous list.

- What is the extent of absence from work in the United Kingdom?
- What does absence from work cost the economy and individual businesses in the United Kingdom annually?
- What are the main causes of absence from work?
- What contribution does work-related sickness make to absence from work?
- Can a strategic approach to occupational health issues improve productivity and profitability?
- How can employees be involved in a strategic approach to occupational health issues?
- How can organisations best invest their resources in occupational health to provide the greatest return?
- To what extent are employees of small businesses more at risk from workplace injuries and ill health than those of larger firms?
- How can the particular problems of small businesses in the occupational health area be met?

Some of these questions may have greater appeal for you than others. Some may suggest how you might refine the research question you are currently working on. Others may suggest ways of formulating a research question that would not be particularly helpful, perhaps inviting simple answers, which are relatively easily established by checking appropriate references, or which invite a simple yes/no answer. Ultimately, you need a clear unambiguous question that relates only to a single issue.

Last, but by no means least, there is a need to evaluate. Looking back at the research projects you have read, how clearly were the research questions stated? Do you think that in some cases they might have been more clearly stated? If so, in what ways? What do you see as the criteria by which the merits of a particular research question might be judged? What does a good research question need to contain? How does this relate to the research question you are currently working with? What have you learnt from this activity, how is it going to take you forward? What do you need to do next? This is a good moment to have a discussion with your prospective supervisor or other experienced researcher about the problems you are experiencing in the final development of your research question – often the most difficult moment of all as so much ultimately depends upon it.

Howard and Sharp (1984) have suggested three techniques for generating research topics:

b. the use of analogy
c. relevance trees
d. morphological analysis.

Hussey and Hussey (2001) have also discussed the latter two.

Howard and Sharp suggest analogy may be useful in the research process in two ways:

(a) if it appears that a particular topic or subject area bears a similarity to another topic or area then this may indicate a potentially useful line of research and
(b) methods of research and/or analysis used in one area may be potentially useful in another.

For example, you may have read about a survey that sought to establish the level of job satisfaction amongst young executives who were members of a particular professional association. This survey might suggest that seeking a challenge in their careers, pay, location, lifestyle, ability to change employers, variety in the job and decision-making opportunities were important to this group. An advertisement seen in newspapers as part of a recruitment drive for officers in one or other of the Armed Services might suggest that a similar survey amongst a group of young officers from one of the Armed Services might throw up some interesting differences and similarities with regard to attitudes to work, lifestyle, and other relationships between work and personal life. The new research might adopt the same approach as the original or might take particular aspects from the first survey that seemed potentially interesting and ask the participants in the new survey to rank various aspects of job satisfaction. In this way, the new research could be of a parallel or derivative kind.

Citing the work of Jantsch (1967), Howard and Sharp suggest that 'relevance trees' 'are excellent models of one of the ways people think about problems'. It is a way of 'developing related ideas from a starting concept'.

A broad starting concept may be used for

(a) suggesting related but different topics
(b) locating some 'niche' topics.

The figure below shows a relevance tree commencing with the broad area of Tourism.

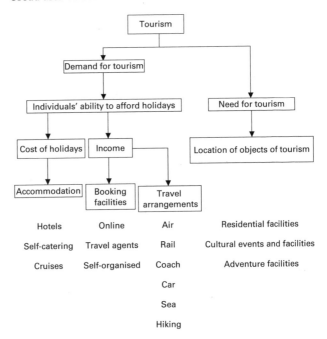

Starting from demand for tourism, two major factors are identified by the researcher, the individuals' ability to afford holidays that is a function of their levels of income and the cost; and their desire to spend a holiday away from home. The latter may be influenced by the location of recreational facilities (sunny beaches), cultural facilities and events (the Cistine Chapel; outdoor operatic performances at Verona), and the possibility of adventure (trekking to Nepal or Tibet; climbing Everest). Matters of cost and location will also be related to the availability of various kinds of accommodation e.g. hotels, cruise ships, self-catering, campsites. Demand may also be influenced by the nature of the booking facilities available – whether it may be done on-line, through travel agents, by post or telephone, or whether people can readily make arrangements for themselves. The ease of travel arrangements by air, sea, car, coach, and rail, walking or hiking may also be a factor. The researcher then identifies the set of variables that might suggest a possible topic e.g. the extent to which people's desire for a tourism-based holiday of a particular kind is affected by the booking facilities available.

Morphological analysis is another approach which Howard and Sharp cite as derived from the work of Jantsch (1967), an approach that is also found in Hussey and Hussey (1997). Morphology is essentially the study of the structure and form of language.

There are three steps in the process.

1. Define the key features of a particular subject.
2. List the various attributes of the factor or ways it can occur.
3. Define all feasible combinations of the attributes.

A table is then drawn up from which the various combinations and possibilities can be analysed to generate what is often a large number of alternative topics, though this may be reduced by restricting your consideration to the particular paradigm in which you are interested.

In the table below you will see that the key factors or dimensions constitute the column headings. The various attributes of the factor are placed within the headings. All the feasible combinations of the attributes are then listed to provide the potential topics. Typically, the major factors are likely to be some combination of aim (what the research is for) or type of research; design or methodology to be employed; and the focus or unit of analysis. This may sound complicated but the table may help to clarify reality.

Aim	Design	Focus
Delineation	Historical analysis	Issue/activity
Explanation	Case study	Profession/interest group
Measurement	Testing of hypothesis	Several organisations
Classification	Comparative analysis	Single organisation
Variable/concept development	Conceptual models	Several departments
Technique development	Mathematical models	One department
Prediction		Several projects
Policy analysis		One project
Theory development		
Type of research	Methodology	Unit of analysis
Exploratory	Cross-sectional studies	An individual
Descriptive	Experimental studies	An event
Analytical	Longitudinal studies	An object
Predictive	Surveys	A body of individuals
Quantitative	Action research	A relationship

Aim	Design	Focus
Qualitative	Case studies	An aggregate
Deductive	Collaborative research	
Inductive	Ethnography	
Applied	Grounded theory	
Basic		

The different kinds of research project can then be chosen by taking an attribute from each of the three columns e.g.

Explanation – Comparative analysis – Several organisations

Descriptive research project – using a survey methodology – using as its unit of analysis a group of army officers

Another kind of research project might be an exploratory project using a case study of a department of a university. Alternatively, a predictive study might use experiments involving individuals to show how sleep deprivation might affect students' examination results.

As a large number of combinations may be possible, it is fortunate that not all the combinations will be feasible e.g. some comparative studies could not be conducted within one department of an organisation. Nevertheless, it is important to confine yourself to the key factors of the chosen subject area as a large number of potential projects may create almost as many difficulties as having too few! In reality, some useful projects may be generated by combining together two or more attributes of one or more than one factor.

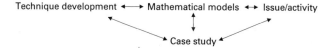

Such a design provides opportunity for testing the performance of techniques which have been developed in an actual situation, and it is thus an attractive proposition.

The great advantage of the morphological approach is that the problem has to be structured and can therefore usefully focus the student whose topic selection tends to be too vague or broad.

An approach advocated by Kane (1984) is to begin with the sentence "I want to find out about" and try to complete it. It is incredibly difficult...

Tutorial

Progress questions

1. What are the essential attributes of a good research question or hypothesis?
2. How might you use analogy to establish a research topic?
3. How might you use relevance trees to establish a research topic?
4. How might you use morphological analysis to establish a research topic?

Discussion points

Some of the techniques discussed above for the generation of research questions will appeal to you more than others. To clarify your thinking about this, discuss the various techniques and advance reasons why you favour some and not others while listening carefully to the views of those with different preferences.

Practical assignment

1. Try completing the sentence "I want to find out about..."
2. Hold a brainstorming session with a small group and note the possible topics that arise.
3. Try developing a relevance tree from a broad area in which you are interested.
4. Use morphological analysis to see if you can generate a number of useful project ideas.

Study and revision tips

1. Whenever you read a research thesis or paper, critique the research question in order to evaluate whether it is as clear and unambiguous as you think it could be. If not, then note the ways in which you think it might be improved.

2. Whenever you read a journal article or research paper or listen to a conference paper, make a note of any suggestions for further research that they contain. Alternatively use one or more of the above techniques, e.g. use analogy to see whether any ideas for research emerge from your consideration of the research discussed.

4 Feasibility

One-minute overview

However clear, interesting and important your research question is, no purpose is served in wasting resources pursuing it if there is any possibility that it may not prove feasible ultimately to bring it to completion. A research project may prove not to be feasible if access is denied to necessary data, locations or individuals, or if the data does not exist, at least in usable form. A lack of resources in the form of time, money or technical skills may also render a project impossible to pursue. Alternatively, it may be that the impossibility of using a desired research design or the high level of risk attached to a particular project approach or outcome (one which may not be that which is desired) may render it inadvisable or personally unacceptable to undertake a particular piece of research. Ethical considerations may also raise doubts about the desirability or feasibility of a particular project, at least in the proposed form.

The final stage of establishing your research question is not yet quite complete. It is necessary to explore the feasibility of undertaking the project successfully. There is no point in having a fascinating and important research question if in practice it does not prove possible to do the research. There are many research questions which would be both interesting and important to research but which cannot be undertaken because it is not feasible to do so. Feasibility can be affected by a number of factors.

1. Access to the necessary data may be difficult or impossible. This problem may take a number of forms.

(i) Access to archives may be denied. In the case of public records e.g. for Government Departments in the United Kingdom, a thirty year rule is imposed preventing access to the records for this length of time. Having said this, there may be ways to obtain at least some of the required information. The Freedom of Information Act may help.

(a) It is always worth asking if access is possible – in the case of Public Records there is a procedure whereby, in some cases, if the information is not deemed to cover anything that is seen as controversial, potentially damaging, or distressing to individuals e.g. an administrative reorganisation, the appropriate scrutiny committee may grant permission subject to certain safeguards. It is also worth remembering that, since devolution, practice may be different in relation to records in England and Wales, Scotland and Northern Ireland.

(b) It may be worthwhile to interview relevant people who may have information. Former Government Ministers or civil servants now retired, for example, may be prepared to discuss the question with you, perhaps on an 'off the record' basis. While this may not be an entirely satisfactory alternative, it may be sufficient for your purposes. It is always worth bearing in mind that people with a grievance about a situation relating e.g. to a former post they held e.g. where they were dismissed or downgraded (unfairly as they saw it) may be very willing to talk (particularly to someone willing or even anxious to listen to their version of events), even though their comments may have to be noted with caution.

However going through this process can be time-consuming and ultimately unprofitable, and unless the project in question has some particular interest for you it may be simpler and less costly in the long run to reject it as not feasible.

(ii) Access may be denied to a necessary site. It has happened that a prospective research student has formulated a perfectly acceptable research question based on human resource practices in a local manufacturing factory, on the assumption that personal friendship with the owners would suffice to ensure access, only to be denied for reasons that were never disclosed. Assumptions about access should never be made in advance! If possible, get your permission in writing. Even then, nothing may be certain. It has happened that the personnel in an organisation change and the successor to a particular post has not regarded himself/herself as bound by the promises given by his/her predecessor. Again, a decision to grant access to records made at one level may be over-turned when the decision reaches a higher level, or when news of what is going on eventually reaches higher echelons who may have genuine grounds for refusal not known to lower levels or who may simply react out of concern or pique that they were not consulted in the first instance. It is better to enlist enthusiastic support for the project at the right levels if at all possible – this is often a better guarantee of securing the necessary ongoing access than personal promises even given in writing or based on the bond of friendship.

2. Even if access is granted or is routinely available, problems may arise which call into question the feasibility of the project.

(i) The data may not be located where you understood it to be. For example, the records may be spread around a number of sites rather than being located centrally. For example, a researcher who wished to obtain data from the school reports for a particular year group in a large comprehensive school was granted access by the Headteacher. However, on arrival at the school, he found that the reports were actually located in the four houses that made up the school which were spread over the city. Furthermore, the heads of house in question had not been informed or consulted and needed to be brought into the situation before data gathering commenced and some did not have the reports conveniently to hand at this time, while others expressed doubts and reservations about the proposed research. It took a matter of some months before this situation was satisfactorily resolved and the data gathering was able to proceed. In some cases, such delay might have proved fatal to a project on account of the time and resource implications.

(ii) The data may not exist in the organisation, or may not exist in the form you had expected or were given to understand existed, or may not exist in a form that is usable for your purposes. In the first case there is little you can do except enquire whether it might be available elsewhere. The author once pursued a set of minutes that was said to exist through a number of suggested keepers until arriving at the eventual location that was very different from the original starting point. In this instance the matter was eventually resolved by some diligent detective work and the willingness and interest of others to take a little time to search their memories for possibilities. In other instances there may be no alternative to deciding the project is not feasible.

Sometimes the data may exist but not in the form you had understood it to be, or in a form which is currently unusable for your purposes. Administrators who may not fully understand your requirements (or who may not have been consulted) will sometimes assure you that the information exists, access is possible and yes – it will tell you all these things, being unaware that the format in which they keep it may not suit your purposes. All you can do is to attempt some assessment of how difficult it would be to turn the data into a usable format and the time and cost involved. Sometimes, it may be possible to copy the data you require and take the copies away and work on them at your leisure rather than in the office hours available. However, the issues of time and resources again come into play, and it is essential to take a rapid decision before you waste too much of these on a project which is ultimately likely to prove not to be feasible.

One of the classic instances where much data can be found but which may not prove to be relevant to a particular research project is the military records of individual soldiers held at the Public Records Office in Kew. The records of many members of the Armed Services in World War I are held at this location, but the records of others have been destroyed.

3. As a related factor to 1 and 2 above, the question of availability of time has to be considered. This may be a matter of the researcher simply attempting to cover too broad a question or pursuing too many questions. In this case it may be possible, relatively easily, to reduce the scale of the project or focus down the number of questions being examined (which is probably desirable in any event). The time available for the completion of a doctoral thesis varies between universities but whatever the maximum permitted, activities such as exploring and defining a suitable problem and writing up may well take half. Bear in mind that some activities can be conducted in parallel, and the data collection and analysis is likely to occupy a period of six to twelve months (longer pro rata for part-time students). A project which is likely to occupy significantly longer than this may therefore be regarded as not feasible for doctoral work. This may rule out some kinds of longitudinal studies e.g. one that proposed to study a cohort of pupils over the five years of their compulsory secondary education in England. The use of alternative research designs such as cross-section studies may sometimes be possible e.g. by focusing on measurements for year one studies and year five studies that are matched by the characteristics you are interested in, but this may critically be a quite different project focused on a different

research question from that originally envisaged and might involve some serious limitations e.g. it would ignore potentially different subject characteristics that might develop over time.

4. The need for specific research and/or technical skills may determine the issue of feasibility. Clearly, a student is more likely to succeed if s/he already possesses the knowledge and skills required to pursue a particular project. Nevertheless, it is often the case that new skills will have to be acquired, most commonly in the area of statistical or content analysis. Sometimes, a corpus of knowledge from a discipline the student has never studied may have to be acquired and if this is not congenial or will take more time and resources than is likely to be available e.g. access to a laboratory to learn how to conduct psychological experiments, then it is probably best to regard the proposed project as not feasible.

5. It must also be considered whether it will be possible to follow the particular research design that the researcher may wish to pursue. One example here would be an experimental design in a scientific area that requires access to some particular kind of laboratory facilities. If the use of such a facility is not available at the university, or in the researcher's own organisation or company, or cannot be negotiated elsewhere, then the project clearly will not be feasible. There are many tempting prospects that might fascinate a student of economics in terms of, for example, pricing policies for a company's commodities, but few commercial organisations are prepared to release pricing data to an outsider or to allow a researcher control over pricing policy for the necessary period of time. In these circumstances it might well be entirely appropriate for a researcher to regard as not feasible a project that did not permit them to use a research design of their choice with which they felt comfortable or in which they felt a particular interest.

6. There needs to be sufficient resources available to cover the requirements of the project, and this principally means finance. This issue has to be resolved before the project is

finally selected, as an inability to finance necessary activities may result in the project collapsing before it has been concluded, meaning not only a waste of the time and resources that have been irretrievably expended but frustration, demoralization and de-motivation for the researcher. Financing may come from the university, a research grant, a sponsor or the researcher, and it is necessary to be totally clear about what will be provided for by these funds and what the researcher will have to find for themselves. In the case of self-financed students, the extent to which activities can be covered may be very limited given the demands upon their income, and this may well incline such students towards essentially simple low-cost research designs, and automatically render some projects not feasible. It is important to remember what the costs of research may include e.g. travel, books (very long term loans from libraries do not always prove practicable), computing, typing if the researcher does not do the word processing themselves, equipment, materials, postage and telephone calls. It is often overlooked, for example, how expensive postal questionnaires can be – often for limited returns. Telephone interviewing has become progressively less expensive over the years, and email is now sometimes a practicable alternative.

7. The researcher has to consider the element of risk involved in the project. This has a number of aspects. The first two have already been mentioned.

   (i) The project may take longer than anticipated.
   (ii) It may prove to be more difficult to complete than expected – or even prove impossible.
   (iii) Some types of research carry an inherently higher risk of failure than others. As Grinyer (1981) cited in Howard and Sharp (1983) suggested, in descending order of risk there is

      (a) pure theory;
      (b) testing of existing theory;
      (c) description of the state of the art;
      (d) specific problem solution.

Interestingly, while the possibility of completing successfully increases down the list, the prospect of making a highly significant and original contribution to knowledge increases as you go up the list. If you are risk averse then from your point of view, a high-risk project may not be feasible personally regardless of the high status academic potential it may offer.

8. Research projects may have several possible outcomes e.g. a null hypothesis may be supported, not supported or an outcome may be inconclusive. Ideally, a researcher should be able to accept any of the outcomes as satisfactory and acceptable. If any of the potential outcomes are not acceptable to the researcher e.g. because it does not match the expectations with which they approached the research, or could not provide the platform the researcher requires, then it may be better to regard the project as not feasible. If symmetry of outcome is not something the researcher can accept in relation to any particular project, then the project really is not feasible in research terms.

9. Projects without an adequate theory base may also not be feasible. Without an adequate theoretical basis to which the research question can be related, it is difficult for a project to make a contribution in the cycle of knowledge development. Observations lead to theory that explains, predicts and raises questions about the phenomenon being observed. Theory also predicts anticipated results or outcomes, and research provides the evidence that supports the theory, or when it does not, suggests the need to amend the theory or provide a new theory.

   The theory base may be associated with the area of study being researched, or it may be drawn from elsewhere, and is a significant factor in establishing the research question and the associated research methods and may also be an important element in the identification of appropriate research topics. All of this suggests that if no relevant theoretical basis can be identified, the project may not be feasible unless you are in the business of establishing new theory – as we have seen already, a high-risk strategy. An example of a topic that might be rejected on the basis of the absence of an appropriate theoretical underpinning would be 'how the juxtaposition of the planets affects human behaviour'. The other situation where the absence of a theoretical framework is not only acceptable but also essential is where the proposed research method involves the use of grounded theory.

One final significant area relating to feasibility may be discussed here, although it might equally be discussed in other parts of the book. This is the important and difficult area of ethical behaviour in research. It is a question that can be too readily overlooked in the pressure and excitement of developing your research question and design.

It may often be the case that your research will involve participants or subjects who are or perceive themselves as being, in a less powerful position than you. In some cases they may be quite vulnerable and open to abuse – even if this is inadvertent and unintentional. However, ethical issues can be very difficult to deal with and there is no universal code of ethics or core values that can offer guidance. There are, nevertheless, some broad general principles that may be followed.

1. No participant should experience physical, mental or social damage as a consequence of the research.
2. Those who are particularly vulnerable – the elderly, children, the mentally ill, the physically handicapped, or other disadvantaged people – should be treated with special care.
3. Your research should not cause physical or environmental damage.
4. Potential participants should be informed of the nature and purpose of the research and their consent should be obtained – informed consent is essential unless some circumstance e.g. mental incapacity rules it out entirely when other appropriate consent from family or legal guardian should be obtained.
5. If anonymity or confidentiality is offered or requested, then any such offer or request must be strictly honoured

subject to any legal requirement that may enforce disclosure.

6. Your research activity must be such as will not damage the reputation of any institution, sponsor or supervisor with whom you are associated.

Many professional bodies provide a statement or code of research ethics for their members, often the work of an ethics committee, and the results of their deliberations may sometimes be discussed and endorsed or amended by the members of the association concerned. The United Kingdom Central Council for Nursing, Midwifery and Health Visiting (1984) have produced a detailed Code of Professional Conduct in relation to research. The World Medical Assembly (1964) has laid down guidelines for doctors working in clinical research. The American Psychological Association (1990) has a similar code of ethical principles for psychologists engaging in research.

The problem with such codes is that there is often some aspect which may not be relevant to a particular context or which in reality may simply not be practicable to follow. Problems may arise because it is not always clear to whom, in your capacity as researcher, you are ultimately responsible.

- The organisation that employs you?
- Those who may have paid for the research?
- Your professional association?
- The participants or subjects in your research?

The difficulty may be that any one or more of these may come into conflict with the others. For example, your sponsors may wish you to press ahead with research which is important to them and for which they have paid, at the expense of the welfare of the participants who might conceivably be damaged by the research e.g. in clinical trials. It is impossible to generalise as circumstances alter cases, but probably your over-riding responsibility is to the participants as in some circumstance the research may have repercussions for them long after you have left the scene. The very least you can do, as

Kane and O'Reilly-de Brun (2001) have pointed out, is not to raise hopes and expectations (of the participants) that you cannot deliver on, and to make the results of your research available to them in some form that is accessible and comprehensible.

In some cases, such as business research, there is no established code of research conduct and the issue of ethical behaviour lies squarely with the individual researcher. Hussey and Hussey (1997:37) point to some of the practical problems that can arise. What do you do if in the course of your research you discover that the company you are observing is failing to take safety measures that would bankrupt the company and render a large number of people in an economically depressed area jobless? Having guaranteed confidentiality to participants, what do you do if in the course of interviewing you discover an employee has been stealing from the firm? If you are engaging in participant observation by joining a work group and participating as if you were an ordinary employee, would you tell the rest of the group that you are, in fact, a researcher, and risk altering the behaviour you are there to observe – where does this leave the principle of informed consent?

It is important also that you never cause a participant loss of dignity e.g. by embarrassing or ridiculing them. Bear in mind that however they may really feel about it, participants may feel that somehow you or your research carries 'authority' and that they are required to participate without any real choice in the decision.

It is, of course, totally unethical to falsify research findings, but it has to be borne in mind that exaggerating or omitting results, being selective in what you present in order to obtain the results you want or to attract attention to your published research is also unethical. However, equally important is the situation that may arise when an individual, group or organisation emerges in a less than favourable light in your research and/or publication. In these circumstances great sensitivity is required in discussing the outcomes and you may consider it courteous to discuss your findings with the participant prior to publication, difficult as this may be.

None of these are easy issues to deal with and in any given set of circumstances a debate would reveal widely differing views about the appropriate course of action. Some researchers might, for example, argue that research codes are too inflexible and cannot be adapted to all situations. There may be, for example, circumstances where to be too open and detailed might compromise your research and that it may be necessary to resort to such behaviour as the covert observation of colleagues in order to collect data. Some would argue it is necessary to inflict a degree of suffering on animals to advance important medical research that will ultimately benefit large numbers of people, or that growing GM crops experimentally under severely limited conditions for research purposes is justified on the grounds that it may ultimately alleviate starvation in some places in the world, and that the small risk of environmental damage is worthwhile. These debates are endless, and the individual researcher can only answer for himself or herself.

Many ethical matters are related to issues of good manners and common consideration e.g. ensuring that individuals and organisations are thanked verbally and in writing for their participation, making available copies of transcripts of interviews or of final reports if these have been requested or copies of any publications that emerge.

Kervin (1992:38) has presented a simple checklist for ethical research which it may be useful to keep by you as you consider your research question and the design of your research project as it covers in a direct way many of the issues that have been raised. It does not, of course, replace any code of research ethics that may have been issued by any professional body relevant to the research you are considering and you should always check to see if any such code exists and what it contains.

1. Will the research process harm participants or those about whom data is gathered (indirect participants)?
2. Are the findings of this research likely to cause harm to others not involved in the research?
3. Are you violating accepted research practice in conducting the research and data analysis, and drawing conclusions?
4. Are you violating community standards of conduct?
5. Perhaps the ultimate test you should apply in any difficult circumstance involving ethical behaviour in the conduct of research is to reverse the perspective and ask yourself – if I were the subject of this research, how would I like the researcher to behave in this situation?

If you have any doubts about the ethical basis of a research proposal, or feel that pursuing the research design you believe is essential to the successful completion of the research would raise serious ethical issues, which might prove insurmountable or might compromise the implementation of the research design, then it is probably better to regard this particular project, at least in this form, as not feasible.

Tutorial

Progress questions

1. What issues of feasibility may be related to questions of access?
2. What resource issues may render a research proposal impossible to pursue?
3. In what ways might the issue of risk cause you to question the desirability of undertaking a particular research project for a PhD?
4. What is the relationship between ethical considerations and feasibility?

Discussion points

1. What ethical considerations would persuade you not to undertake a research project which was adequately supported in terms of resource provision?
2. What personal considerations of risk attached to a particular research project would cause you to conclude it was not feasible?

Practical assignments

1. List the possible research questions you have been considering and examine their feasibility in terms of access, resources and risk factors.
2. For your list of possible research questions consider

    (i) any ethical issues that may arise and how you might deal with them and
    (ii) whether any professional codes of ethics might be relevant to the conduct of the research.

Study and revision tips

1. Make a list of any professional or equivalent bodies that might be related to your proposed research and establish whether they have drawn up codes of research ethics.

2. Examine the research proposals you are considering and make a list of the research resources of all kinds that would be required in each case. Check whether there is evidence that the resources are, or could be made, available.

5   The Research Proposal

One-minute overview

The research proposal is an important document whether or not it is required by your institution, as it serves to justify and describe the proposed study. It indicates what you intend to do, and why and how you want to do it. It provides assurance that the research design and methods chosen will effectively address the problem. It will clarify your thoughts and allow others to comment constructively on the project. It normally contains a literature review, a problem statement, and an indication of the research method and mode of analysis. It may have been preceded by a number of topic analyses relating to different possible topics for research. Topic analyses provide some indication of whether the resource demands of some topics, the possible failure to attract a supervisor may render a particular topic improbable or whether one topic is particularly attractive to you personally. The ultimate choice of topic may be determined by the probability of successful completion as indicated by a list of proposed chapters and the major activities relating to each contending topic. The inability to provide such lists may suggest an impossible topic. Also important is the likelihood that the examiners will accept the completed thesis on the basis that each possible outcome will contribute to knowledge and will be accepted as so doing by the examiners. An expansion of the topic analysis can then be used to facilitate the research proposal, and provide the basis for the structure of chapters in the thesis.

The next step in your research progress is to submit whatever is required by your institution as a formal research proposal. This is a very variable document, and there is no universally agreed format. Some institutions provide a very rigid and detailed framework to be completed – sometimes to the point where it becomes difficult to fit some perfectly valid and interesting proposals within the structure – the 'one size fits all' approach can present problems of its own.

Proposals may then be subjected to scrutiny by a sub-committee, which then has to report back to a larger research committee. Such committees may include members who are not knowledgeable about your particular area of research or your research paradigm or research method and tend to look for specific answers that may not be relevant to your proposal. Some scientists or engineers may have difficulties in coming to terms with the concept of Grounded Theory. The questions thus raised can be a source of irritation and frustration but have to be dealt with by citing appropriate references to the literature in support of the aspect of the proposal that is being challenged. It is important to remember that these issues are usually raised in all sincerity and with the intention of improving the proposal and eliminating uncertainties. Naïve questions can actually be useful – they may force you to think with greater clarity about the point in question and to explain it in a way that is more readily comprehended and even thus increase your own understanding of it – which can be helpful when you come to discuss this issue in your thesis.

In some institutions there is no prescribed framework and the proposal can be written very much as you wish, subject always to the need to cover some essential elements, and may be subject only to acceptance by the prospective supervisor, although this situation seems to have become less common with the establishment of quality assurance agencies in the United Kingdom. Whatever model of proposal submission confronts you, it is important to turn it to your advantage and derive benefit from the otherwise tiresome process of drawing up the appropriate document. Regard it as a positive contribution to your research progress rather than as being the negative chore many people see it as being.

Rudestam and Newton (2001) have described the research proposal as "an action plan that justifies and describes the proposed study". They point to the great importance of this stage in the overall process of thesis writing, and suggest that "an approved proposal means more than half of the work of the dissertation has been completed". Without going this far it is easy to see that being able to meet the following questions advanced by Rudestam and Newton in relation to research proposals would be an enormous step forward and would be the result of some hard initial thinking.

1. Is the question clear and researchable and will the answer to the question extend knowledge in your field of study?
2. Have you located your question within a context of previous study that demonstrates that you have mastered and taken into consideration the relevant background literature?
3. Is the proposed method suitable for exploring your question?

So, what is a research proposal? It is a detailed statement of

- What you intend to do
- Why you want to do it
- How you will go about it

(Burnard and Morrison, 1990)

It provides assurance about your ability to successfully complete the project and that the research design and methods you have chosen will effectively address the problem identified. It also

(a) assists you in clarifying your thoughts and methods
(b) allows others to comment on the project and provide additional insights.

The process of writing a research proposal is seldom easy, is likely to require a number of drafts, and may involve a request for changes from any scrutiny committee. Any such requests must be met either by incorporating the changes in such a way as to maximise any positive impact they may have or by seeking to introduce them in a way that meets the requirements of the committee but which is not going to adversely affect your research plans. You should never refuse to make required changes – this is likely to merely result in the outright rejection of the proposal. It may be possible to offer a further explanation that causes the committee to modify its view on some proposed changes, but ultimately graceful acceptance is the only realistic option.

In spite of what was said about the diversity of research proposals and the associated requirements, there are some common elements which may be identified in good proposals, and even where the aspects discussed below are not specifically required in your institution's document, it is well worthwhile drawing up your own document which covers a wider spectrum of relevant points and issues. Essentially, a proposal will contain the following elements:

(a) a literature review
(b) a problem statement
(c) the research method and mode of data analysis.

In some cases, the submission of the research proposal will have been preceded by the preparation of a number of topic analyses relating to different possible topics for research. These topic analyses are essentially short – no more than four pages maximum. If the institution in question does not provide for a formal consideration of topic analyses by some scrutiny committee i.e. there are no formal documents provided for the prospective student to complete, then the student may construct them for him or herself. Again, the precise content of any topic analysis may vary according to the subject and circumstances. Howard and Sharp (1983) and Davis and Parker (1997) have particularly devoted some attention to topic analysis. Some of the following elements are likely to be common to most topic analyses:

1. the hypothesis, question, problem or research objective;
2. the significance of the research – why it is important and interesting;

3. the theoretical base or conceptual framework;
4. prior research in the topic area;
5. the research paradigm and probable research method or approach;
6. possible outcomes of the research and the value and importance of these.

What is required at this stage is a succinct statement under each heading.

Davis and Parker (1997:83–85) provide a useful example of a topic analysis and make some relevant brief comments about each section.

Section 1 often causes problems. While its focus is clearly what the thesis will deal with, the issue of the hypothesis can cause concern. An hypothesis may be defined as 'a single statement that attempts to explain or to predict a single phenomenon' (Simon, 1968:37). This may be contrasted with a theory that may be defined as 'a process of organizing reality into systematically identified relationships among variables to explain and make predictions about phenomena' (Feldman, 1990). Theories are developed and tested through empirical observations and research which give rise to generalizations. The attraction of formulating an original hypothesis lies in the possibility that if supported it will clearly provide an original contribution to knowledge. However, it is frequently the case that no such hypothesis can be established. Any hypotheses that are identified may merely be trivial and not contribute significantly to knowledge. Sometimes it is therefore more useful when the topic cannot be dealt with appropriately by the use of an hypothesis to state the question or problem simply and clearly. In some circumstances it may be appropriate to incorporate more than one hypothesis.

Section 2 is very important in relation to doctoral degrees. The research indicated has to have sufficient intrinsic value to be worth doing. It may be possible to quote some authority in the field on the intrinsic value or the need for this research. Bear in mind here that an original contribution does not have to be groundbreaking. It will probably 'be rather limited in its scope and indeed should be' (Phillips and Pugh, 1994:35).

Section 3. Here, the theoretical or conceptual frameworks derived from previous research from which the hypothesis or question is established, are identified. This provides the underlying rationale for the research and the investigation of the hypothesis or problem.

Section 4. In the topic analysis this section need not be of enormous length but should identify the significant previous research which leads towards this topic.

Section 5. This section is of great significance as it suggests the research paradigm and the research methods within that paradigm that the student is proposing to use. While the statement needs to discuss this issue with some degree of precision e.g. the kind of survey that is being proposed, whether a population frame is known to exist for sampling purposes, and the mode of data analysis that is likely to be most appropriate, detail is not necessary at this stage. You cannot be expected to have formulated a draft questionnaire at this stage, although you might be expected to know whether the existing state of knowledge would lend itself to the construction of a viable questionnaire. Any alternative methods which might be possible, or which might have been considered and rejected should be included here, with reasons for their rejection, if applicable.

Section 6. This can be a crucial section in determining whether the topic is worth pursuing. If only one out of three or four possible outcomes is likely to provide a successful thesis, then this might suggest a topic which would carry a potentially high risk of failure and one which might not be worth pursuing to proposal stage.

Remember the purpose of the topic analysis:

1. to clarify your thinking about the various possibilities;
2. to eliminate unsuitable projects or research that is not feasible for whatever reason;
3. to stimulate further thoughts and ideas;
4. to suggest alternatives;
5. to invite comment from others.

It will become apparent that the resource demands of some topics e.g. time or cost is too great for the topic to be viable. In some cases no prospective supervisor may be willing to provide supervision. It may be that one topic stands out from the others for whatever reasons. It may appeal to you personally and is likely to be completed within the time, finance and other resources available. Sometimes, there may be two or more topics left that might be acceptable. Here, the decision is necessarily a personal one depending on the degree to which you are risk-averse or willing to choose a 'risky' topic which has the possibility of a highly significant outcome but also the considerable risk of failure; whether you wish to use the thesis as the basis for further research; and your perception of its likely impact on your career as well as on your personal life in the immediate term.

If the choice is not resolved by these factors, Davis and Parker (1997) suggest that each topic might be assessed for selection purposes by what they describe as 'two probabilities'.

1. What is the probability of successful completion? To answer this question they suggest making two lists for each topic

   (a) the chapters you expect to be contained in the thesis
   (b) the major activities you expect to have to undertake to complete the thesis together with an estimate of the time you expect each activity to take.

They suggest that if you are unable to do these two things or it is very difficult then this suggests that completion may be difficult. 'If it cannot be planned, it probably cannot be done.'

2. The probability that the examiners will accept the completed thesis. This depends on :

   (a) the probability that each of the possible outcomes will make a contribution to knowledge

   (b) the probability that the examiners, especially the external examiner, will accept each of these results as contributing to knowledge.

(Davis and Parker, 1997)

Once a topic has been selected, the next step is to expand the relevant topic analysis into a research proposal, which is essentially a work plan for the thesis. The research proposal does two things.

1. It shows the need for, and importance of, the study.
2. It demonstrates that the researcher has, or can acquire, the skills and resources necessary to complete the project.

It should be borne in mind that although this is a 'final' document in the sense that the appropriate scrutinizing body will formally approve this version of the research proposal, it remains a working document which may well be modified on a number of occasions as the work proceeds.

The principal additions that are likely to have to be made to the topic analysis to turn it into a research proposal are:

(a) a summary, of one or two paragraphs in length
(b) a proposed work schedule (necessarily tentative)
(c) a provisional description of the proposed structure and detail of the chapters the thesis is likely to contain.

Other areas of the topic analysis will need to be expanded e.g. the prior research and literature review, and the research methods. Overall, the length of a research proposal may vary from 10 to 30 pages, with 15 pages probably being a reasonable target. One common danger is the temptation to make the proposal too long e.g. by including a lengthy literature review. If you feel that a literature review of significant length is required then it may be appropriate to attach it as an appendix, bearing in mind that putting anything into an appendix may be seen as an invitation to people to not read it!

The structure of the research proposal will probably look something like this.

1. Summary or Abstract
2. The research problem with hypothesis or hypotheses or research question
3. The interest and importance of the research
4. The theoretical or conceptual frameworks
5. The literature review incorporating previous research
6. The research paradigm and the research methods
7. The limitations and key assumptions
8. The value of the possible outcomes as contributions to knowledge
9. The proposed structure and contents of the chapters in the thesis

The Summary or Abstract is essentially a brief outline of what the thesis is about, what is proposed to be do and how it is to be done.

The research problem, hypothesis or question will probably be substantially the same as in the topic analysis, although there may be some expansion or further clarification, but it is primarily essential that it remains sharp and clear.

The interest and importance of the research is also likely to remain unchanged from the topic analysis.

The theoretical or conceptual frameworks may need some expansion e.g. a more powerful justification for the use of these concepts or frameworks or some critique of the concepts or frameworks that recognises their potential weaknesses and limitations.

The literature review with an emphasis on previous research is likely to have to be expanded beyond that contained in the topic analysis. By this time you will almost certainly have accumulated additional references from your ongoing study and it should by now be sufficiently comprehensive to have incorporated all the significant references that are likely to ultimately be included in the thesis. If the references on previous work are at all extensive then a summary will be necessary, particularly if a first draft goes beyond five pages. The possibility of using an appendix may be available, as mentioned above, but should probably be avoided if at all possible. It may not be read, or may be regarded as a means of circumventing any word or page limitations placed upon the research proposal.

The research paradigm and the research methods will almost certainly need to be expanded as the research proposal needs to be as explicit on these matters as it can be at this stage. The method of data collection should be explained and justified, any agreed access indicated, and any population frame that has been located for sampling purposes should be mentioned. In a questionnaire survey, the derivation of possible questions and their sources, the nature of the various kinds of questions to be asked, with examples if possible, and the mode of analysis, should all be included. Sampling procedures or procedures to be used in an experimental design, together with apparatus, instruments and methods of observation and data collection should be explained as appropriate. The location of any observation sites, with the subjects and frequency of observations should be mentioned if relevant. There will, of course, be many things that may not be known at this time and many changes in what is anticipated are likely to occur, and all that can be done is to indicate intentions as clearly as possible. If there are some important decisions relating to the implementation of the research methods that have not yet been determined these should be clearly stated.

The limitations and key assumptions are important in placing boundaries around the thesis and defining what the work will cover. This may prevent you from attempting too much (a common danger) or from wandering into interesting by-ways which emerge during the course of the research but which do not contribute directly to addressing the problem which is the focus of the study. In describing the limits of what you intend to do, or the assumptions you have made which have guided the way the experiment will be conducted, or the model or framework applied or how observations will be undertaken, be explicit and indicate where appropriate, what the study will not do.

The value of the possible outcomes (all of them whether hoped for or not) as contributions to knowledge will probably remain much as in the topic analysis, unless the need for further detail becomes apparent.

The provisional structure and content of the chapters gives further definition to the thesis, and each chapter can be briefly described (no more than a short paragraph on each) without too much detail. It is essentially the structure and the relationship between the chapters that need to be highlighted and made as specific as is reasonably possible at this stage.

It may be appropriate to consider at this point the structure of the chapters in a 'typical' thesis. There is, of course, room for flexibility in the structure according to the needs of the particular thesis. This may be particularly the case in the presentation of the results where there is, for example, a large number of statistical tables involved, and these may need to be grouped broadly according to subject or topic across two or three related chapters. It may also be necessary in such a situation to consider whether the discussion of the results needs to follow each particular set of tables, or whether it is best left to one major subsequent chapter. These matters can only be determined in the light of the particular thesis.

Howard (1978), Howard and Sharp (1983) and Davis and Parker (1997) all present a similar list of chapters. A more detailed discussion of the contents of the structure and contents of the thesis can be found later in the book.

1. The Introduction. This locates the specific research question in its general problem area, suggests why it is interesting and important, mentions briefly the previous

research from which it follows, the research paradigm and methods followed by the thesis, any important assumptions which have been made together with the limitations of the thesis, and the contribution to knowledge which it makes.

2. The Literature Review, which will include a survey of previous research (if any). This may be very limited or very extensive depending on your thesis. If it is very extensive, then two chapters on this theme may be justified with perhaps one of them concentrating on the theoretical or conceptual frameworks involved. In any event, this chapter may also include a discussion of the relevant theoretical or conceptual frameworks within which the research and in particular the discussion of the results and the conclusions may be placed. It is this part of the thesis which places the research in its context and background and furnishes evidence to the effect that this research is your own original work and is not a mere duplication of someone else's previous efforts.

3. The Research Methods. This will justify, describe and critique the research methods that were employed, whether these involved an experimental design, a simulation model, some kind of measuring technique – perhaps an intelligence test or personality test (or a series of such tests), observational methods, a questionnaire survey, an interviews, or documentary/content analysis. This chapter effectively describes how the research was done.

4. The Results of the Research. Here the data arising from the application of the research methods described earlier are presented, the documentary or historical analysis is defined, or comparative case studies, for example, are explained.

5. The Analysis of the Results. It has already been suggested that in some cases this may be incorporated into the previous chapter, or alternatively an analysis of the results may be accompanied by a discussion of their meaning and significance in relation to the theoretical or conceptual frameworks employed. This very much depends on the circumstances of the thesis. It can readily be seen that this chapter represents, in some sense, the crux of the thesis.

6. Summary, Conclusions, Recommendations. Here, a summary of the results may be referred back to the Literature Review and the theoretical and conceptual frameworks to see how these are inter-related with the result of the research, and questions may be identified for further research arising from the results.

The preparation of a structure of chapters in this way should help to focus your mind particularly in defining the objective of a completed and successful thesis.

By this time, you should have in hand a document on which the supervisor or scrutiny committee can base a reasonable judgment that the project should now be able to proceed with every probability of a successful outcome. At the very worst, the research proposal should attract constructive criticism such that a revised and amended version is likely to be accepted at the next opportunity.

Tutorial

Progress questions

1. What are the purposes and benefits in preparing a research proposal?
2. What questions need to be answered in the preparation of a research proposal?
3. What principal elements will a research proposal contain?
4. What is the purpose of a topic analysis?
5. What common elements are likely to be found in most topic analyses?

Discussion points

1. Would you use time and resources to prepare a research proposal if your institution did not require it?
2. What feedback on your research proposal would you look for from your scrutiny committee?

Practical assignments

1. Prepare a draft topic analysis for any topic which you may be considering and relate it to resource demands and any personal appeal it may have for you.
2. If the topic analyses do not resolve your choice of topic, apply the 'two probabilities' as suggested by Davis and Parker.
3. Prepare a draft research proposal for the topic or topics that you feel are real possibilities, ensuring that it answers the questions posed by Rudestam and Newton.

Study tips and revision

1. Look back over the essential elements in a topic analysis and ensure that your topic analyses meet the essential criteria indicated in the chapter.
2. Look back over the essential elements in a research proposal and ensure that your proposal(s) will meet the relevant criteria for your institution, and answer the questions posed in the chapter.

One-minute overview

Planning is necessary in doctoral research to ensure time and other resources are used in an optimal way. Without it, the consequences may be a lack of progress, frustration and demoralization. Planning focuses on the management of the research and its separate but inter-related elements. It also takes account of difficulties that may arise both within the research context and outside it e.g. family or personal problems. Network planning is one approach to managing research projects, which provides a basis of control together with flexibility to meet uncertainties. A Gantt chart may be drawn up from the network analysis to facilitate smoothing out demands on resources and organizing non-critical activities in order to reduce demands at critical times. It is also important to link a planning schedule with your budget as part of your research framework. Planning also assists the establishment of a 'productive mindset' and in documenting progress.

So now you have had you research proposal accepted. What is the next step? You need to establish a plan for the progress of your research. This is a wise and useful investment of time. As General Eisenhower is reputed to have said "The plan is nothing. Planning is everything." Any plan you may make will certainly have to undergo changes as the project progresses. It is the process of planning that provides various important elements in stimulating the researcher to make progress, enabling problems to be resolved, priorities to be re-assessed and limited resources to be managed effectively.

Why is it necessary to plan a research project? Are there not too many uncertainties involved that make planning both difficult and futile? It is important largely because scarce resources need to be used in an optimal way, and the most precious of these scarce resources is your time. An absence of planning is often the source of a lack of progress, a duplication of work, frustration and demoralization.

A planning framework performs useful functions for the researcher.

1. It flags up to the researcher that difficult problems have arisen.
2. It motivates the researcher as it offers the encouragement of seeing short-term goals achieved, and cumulative successes create a positive climate towards completion.
3. It identifies necessary or desirable courses of action.
4. It identifies potential difficulties or hidden dangers.
5. It serves as the foundation for control of the project.

A research plan can take many forms and individual researchers will have their own preferences in terms of format and degree of detail, but there are some essentials that need to be addressed whatever the style of planning adopted.

The plan itself needs to provide a means of evaluating the progress of the project on the basis of a schedule of activities which has been established as a result of a comprehensive analysis of what needs to be done – a vague collection of a number of estimates of the time that will be involved in loosely organised research activities is not sufficient.

Planning in this context is not concerned with the subject matter of the research. It does focus on the following.

1. How the research project is to be managed.
2. The establishment of separate but necessarily inter-related elements that are all required for the completion of the research. These elements are all necessary, but are not of equal importance. Nevertheless, every activity has to be planned and located according to where it needs to take place in the research schedule.

The focus of planning needs to be on the following purposes:

1. clarifying the aims and objectives of the researcher;
2. defining what needs to be done to achieve the aims;
3. establishing the order in which these activities are to be undertaken;
4. establishing a critical path with crucial 'milestones' in the progress of the research where certain activities need to be brought together;
5. indicating points where reviews of the progress could suitably be undertaken;
6. re-assessing the research plan when the plan identifies the need;
7. estimating the time involved between the successive milestones;
8. identifying the points when the various milestones will be reached in order to measure progress;
9. ensuring the effective use of crucial scarce resources, particularly the researcher's time;
10. ongoing definition and redefinition of priorities during the course of the research;
11. guiding the purposes of the research to improve the projects of a timely and successful submission.

This may seem to be a complex and elaborate list, but the need for detailed and painstaking planning increases as resources become scarcer, and few researchers have excessive amounts of money and other important resources, particularly time, such that careful use is not required. Some research activities are also of an unusual or non-routine nature that may give rise to problems that cannot readily be foreseen, and this requires careful forward planning.

It must be remembered that the acceptance of the research proposal implies that the research project can be completed within the time allowed, and that the potential conflict between the creative production of original research and working within even self-imposed deadlines will be resolved so that the limitations of time imposed by the institution and your own circumstances will be met. It is for this reason that a structure has to be applied to the work such that it assumes priority over unstructured and less significant activities. Some researchers commence the working week with some time – perhaps an hour – set aside for planning and setting out the tasks that will fill the week, with estimated times to be taken up by each activity. It may be suggested also that it is worth providing more tasks for the week than are likely to be completed, putting them in order of priority. This means that should it be the case, for any reason, that it is not possible to pursue some of the allocated activities that week, then alternatives are at hand to fill the vacant slots. In the following week's planning session, the amount of time actually spent on each individual task can be compared with the time that was allotted, and so the cost-effectiveness of the various activities in terms of time can be judged and decisions made about the future allocation of time for these tasks.

It should also be acknowledged that over the period of three to five years or more you are involved in establishing a research project, undertaking the research and writing up the thesis, as well as preparing its defence, there will inevitably be times when personal problems e.g. your health or that of a member of your close family, will cause interruptions.

Other difficulties may arise from problems with computer technology, delays in being able to meet with supervisors and in binding the thesis – assuming you can do your own typing on a word processor and do not have to experience the delays and expense in employing a typist that may otherwise cause problems. In other words, realistically, if you intend to write up your thesis over a period of, say, twelve months, the work actually needs to be programmed within a nine-month period in order to take account of any problems that may arise. One benefit of allocating nine months rather then twelve is that any tendency to procrastination may be reduced, and procrastination can readily take over if you are not vigilant.

Another source of delay may arise from wider family problems. It is easy to become totally but unconsciously absorbed in the business of producing a thesis and overlook

1. the effect the 'grind' of the work can have on your own health, given the long hours you may find yourself working, with adverse consequences for the quality of your work as exhaustion sets in;

2. the need for recreation – including holidays and breaks which are indeed necessary – if other members of your family, particularly children, are involved.

One way to deal with these problems is for you to block out a particular time in the week for family recreation and for social activities with friends. These need to be factored into your planning, and should not be looked upon as a waste of time or as a diversion from the principal current objective of your life. It is a way of maintaining the vital quality of your physical and mental health and your personal relationships, which ultimately will benefit the quality of your work.

Howard and Sharp (1983) have advocated an approach called network planning. It is argued that this

(a) serves as a basis of control over projects whatever their lengths and these will inevitably differ;

(b) provides the flexibility to meet the inevitable uncertainties which flow from research.

The technique itself was derived from the successful use of network analysis techniques in planning and controlling

(i) industrial research projects and (ii) complex construction processes.

The application of the technique was further stimulated by the development of the computer that was used to bring together the multiplicity of processes and tasks involved in large-scale construction work.

The techniques of network analysis are designed to assist in

(a) planning and

(b) controlling situations where there is a wide range of activities which it is very difficult to deal with, particularly in terms of the relationships between these activities. They are particularly useful where the researcher has little experience of managing projects and has not yet developed his/her own system for dealing with management issues.

Even where it is not considered appropriate to follow the model itself, the methods involved in network planning as applied to a research project will provide guidance in highlighting the major aspects of the planning process. Network methods can be used to plan and control a research project of any size, and nowadays can be supported by network programs available in computers to which most researchers will have ready access. Regardless of the number of activities involved, it is essential that the network itself is drawn manually, leaving the analysis to the computer to provide the times of commencement and conclusion of the various activities, as well as an indication of any room for manoeuvre available in the form of 'slack' or unfilled time which can be used for emergency measures if required.

The following is a list of necessary activities involved in the process of network planning.

1. Determine the objectives.
2. Identify and list (in any order) the activities that need to be carried out.
3. Order the activities. Establish for every activity those activities that precede it, those that follow it, and those which may be undertaken concurrently.
4. Draw the network.
5. Estimate the time needed to complete each activity.
6. Analyse the network using the completion times.
7. Check the resources and draw up the schedule.
8. Replan as necessary.

Howard and Sharp (1983:49–63) have discussed these activities in detail and their recommendations should be studied and implemented as appropriate.

You should never commit all of any resource to the thesis, particularly your own time. In practice, about 80% of any resource could be committed, leaving some 20% as the contingency available. This will have implications for the length of your working day and you must assess the significance of this for yourself in considering your network plan. Over an extended period, an effective working week of 40 hours would seem appropriate, giving enough leeway for an increase in the short term if this should prove necessary. This also has the merit of avoiding excessive hours being worked except when totally necessary, and even then the number of weeks for which this continues should be constrained and be followed by some suitable period of relaxation.

There may be, of course, some elements in the schedule that impact resources lying outside your power of control. You are not able normally to influence the timing of lectures or seminars, the dates of conferences or when experimental equipment will be available. These factors can often be dealt with by using a Gantt chart to adjust some of the float, and are more easily dealt with by the use of a magnetic board or maintaining the Gantt chart on your personal computer so that you can print out any adjustments as necessary. A Gantt-type chart may be drawn up directly from the network analysis. It may assist in identifying a number of issues.

1. Float is easily identified and enables you to smooth out demands on resources.
2. Given that the major resource is your time, non-critical activities can be organised to reduce demands on your time at critical points.

If it proves to be the case that the various activity floats are insufficient to meet the demands on your time, then the only solution may be to postpone the submission of the thesis. In coming to a conclusion about the likelihood of this happening, you should ensure that your resources are not over-stretched.

Milestones in research

You might use a marker relating to the current week in order to get a clear idea of progress and where you are in the research. You could also colour code the duration of each activity, filling in the bar proportionately with this colour as the work progresses on this activity.

This will provide an instant update on where you are ahead of schedule, where you are falling behind, where there may be slippage in dates you are working to and above all, provide the necessary motivation as you can see the work progressing in tangible form.

Milestone events or benchmarks can be seen designated. At these very significant points, progress should normally be reviewed, particularly as they will often occur at the end of a sequence of activities where uncertainty of outcome was present. At these natural points in the research project it is essential to establish what progress has been made and whether the network plan is still viable as it stands or whether some amendments are required. In the ordinary course of events, milestones will come up at fairly frequent intervals, but in the event that for some reason there is a gap of, say, three months between two successive such events, then you should proceed with a major review of your progress through the network in any case. A milestone or three month review is certainly something that should be discussed with your supervisor, and with other interested parties such as fellow researchers, if at all possible.

Carrying out the research: the use of networks

The networks you are likely to draw will probably be of the relatively less complex kind, and you should be able to redraw as necessary without great difficulty, but if they are to be used and to be of value throughout the project they must be at least a very close approximation of how you see the series and sequences of activities which you are going to follow until you reach the conclusion of your research with the submission of the thesis.

To abandon planning and your network once you start actual research work on your selected topic is to invite problems, and your reappraisals resulting from your reviews of your progress as you proceed will point you in the direction of the necessary re-planning.

By now you may well be thinking that the use of network analysis is both complex and unnecessarily burdensome, and that it is not for you. Before finally dismissing the possibility of using this technique, it is suggested that you examine the advantages of the technique as advanced by two of the principal proponents of its merits.

"(a) The emphasis on rigorous planning, schedules and milestones is a notion to which students with limited time at their disposal should become accustomed.

(b) If a network is used to plan a research study there is little likelihood that significant activities that need to be anticipated will be overlooked.

(c) The levelling out of major peaks of demand on the researcher's time or the elimination of infeasible requirements for other resources may be possible.

(d) In the event that planning indicates that, despite the rough estimates included within the research proposal, there would seem to be little prospect of achieving an acceptable completion date major or minor changes to plan may be made.

(e) The efforts of the student will be focused on the achievement of the next milestone, thus providing a way of regularly reviewing progress as the project unfolds and identifying situations in which re-planning is necessary.

(f) Motivation is generated by visual evidence of tasks competed, together with an awareness of the extent to which endeavour should be increased.

(g) The network and the associated charts provide an excellent basis for communicating to others what activities remain to be completed and how they are linked, achievement to date and the schedule the researcher proposes to follow. The very fact that the supervisor is aware of progress is a considerable aid to keeping on schedule." (Howard and Sharp, 1983:64)

Kane (1984) links the preparing of a schedule and a budget as the ultimate step in establishing your research framework. This is important in

(a) determining whatever you are going to need to obtain financial help or whether you will need someone to help you with the work – this can be crucially important in applying for a research grant or scholarship for your PhD;
(b) deciding to limit the scope of your research question further in order to save both time and other resources, particularly money.

Two elements comprise preparing the schedule and budget.

A. Kane proposes preparing an order of tasks as they might appear in your schedule list. These might be:

1. prepare Research Statement
2. prepare research outline
3. prepare Research Design
4. perform research
5. analyse research findings
6. prepare research report.

These tasks must be broken down into the necessary separate tasks e.g. under Perform research, if you are using questionnaires, you must provide time for devising the questions; producing a draft of the questionnaire; asking people who might be potentially useful to comment on the draft; change the draft if necessary as a result of this consultation; undertake a pilot run; reviewing the results from the pilot; redrafting the questions and/or layout; run a further pilot if necessary; make any further amendments needed; print off the required number of completed questionnaires;

print off the required number of covering letters; obtain the requisite number of envelopes of the right size for dispatch and return; address the envelopes (or arrange for it to be done); make arrangements about return postage; stuff the addressed envelopes with the letter, questionnaire and return envelope; deliver them to the post – and all before you receive back a single completed questionnaire for analysis.

B. Estimate the required amount of time you think will be needed for each of the tasks you have listed. Each task can then be represented on a Gantt-type chart using a horizontal line across a calendar to provide the project schedule. As pointed out earlier, it is very difficult, particularly when you are inexperienced, to make a sound judgement of the time each task is likely to take. One sensible approach is to ask experienced researchers roughly how long they think a particular task is likely to take, drawing upon their experience e.g. transcribing the notes of an hour long interview can easily take three hours. However carefully you plan the time allocated to each task, Kane suggests you add an additional one-third to it in order to be as sure as you can that you have allowed enough time. On the basis of the various allotments of time you have made to the undertaking of the multitude of different tasks, you can prepare your research budget. Shading in the months on the calendar in your project budget will indicate when expenses or charges will have to be met, based on the assumption that you have to pay out the money in the same month that the activity for which it pays takes place. This may not always be the case – you may be billed for some computer work, for example, in the following month after it was undertaken. In this case put the expense in the month in which it occurs. The costs of an activity or task that continues over a period of longer than one month can be divided equally over each of the months involved unless there is a compelling reason for payments to be made unequally.

Brause (2000) in addition to pointing out the necessity to schedule your research times (including times when you will have access to specific resources) highlights two other interesting aspects of planning.

1. Establishing what she calls a 'productive mindset', which she argues involves reducing the tensions by limiting the pressures both outsiders and you will place upon yourself and in this way freeing yourself to do the work on the project.

   Write down any casual thoughts which come into your head relating to the research as they occur, so always have the necessary writing materials to hand, and record a note on the idea wherever it happens and as your brain continues to turn over thoughts on the project so that you are given a clear reminder of the notion when you come to work on the thesis again.

2. Documenting your progress, which is very helpful in getting beyond what can be the frustration early on in the process, when it seems that nothing in the way of progress is happening. This will involve the kind of checklist previously noted under network planning and may involve a repetition of similar activities which inevitably recur in the process of research, but with the additional dimension of noting specifically how you have made progress in moving your thesis towards its submission.

In scheduling the times for thesis research, Brause advocates a flexible approach to planning. She recognises that even if you had planned to allocate time to work on the thesis every day in a given week it is likely that other commitments and responsibilities will almost certainly eat into that time, and goes on to urge that you do not focus on what did not happen. She suggests that you should be adamant that, as a minimum, you are going to keep to your personally drafted schedule, but that otherwise you should exploit any additional time that becomes available e.g. an unexpected free afternoon if the mood takes you! Some, on the other hand would say do not use such time for your thesis. Ultimately, you must do what your instinct tells you suits you – and what works for one would be inappropriate for someone else. What is required is realistic adjustment of your expectations and your schedule so that you can meet both your agenda and your responsibilities. This has also to take into account when you can get (or perhaps more significantly cannot get) access to necessary resources for your thesis e.g. you will need to make alternative arrangements if your institution's library closes for several weeks one summer for refurbishment or transfer to a new building. You will need to find alternative access to a library that may be less conveniently located or pursue other avenues of progress on the thesis during this time, or both if the less convenient location of the alternative library limits your visits.

Essentially, you should always have a good idea of what your next step will be, and this will keep you focused immediately ahead on the tasks to be done and on moving towards the goal of timely submission of the thesis (Brause, 2000:88–90).

Tutorial

Progress questions

1. What functions does a planning framework perform for a researcher?
2. What does planning focus on in the research context?
3. What necessary activities are involved in the process of network planning?
4. What steps are involved in (a) the planning phase and (b) the effectuation phase of the process model of research planning?

Discussion points

1. What benefits would you look for from the planning of a research project?
2. How do you feel you would want to go about planning you research project? Why would you want to do it this way?

Practical assignments

1. Draw up a draft plan for any research project(s) you are considering.
2. Attempt to draw a preliminary version of a network ordering the activities you are likely to have to engage in for your project(s).
3. Draw a provisional Gantt chart to provide a project schedule.

Study tips and revision

1. Revisit the draft plans, networks and schedules you have drawn up for your project(s) and identify any problem areas where the required resources, including time, may present difficulties or uncertainties. Consider how you might deal with these.
2. Consider how far the draft plans, networks and schedules you have drawn up meet the functions and objectives of planning indicated at the beginning of this chapter.

7 **Organizing Your Data**

One-minute overview

Good record-keeping is central to organising data in usable and time saving form. Essential details should not be cut down on in your notes, as your recall will be limited. Speedy and accurate transcription of information is necessary, and should be routinised as far as possible. Recording also needs to be organised to cover a wide range of situations and sources. Notes should be recorded in a standardised notebook with each notebook and page appropriately numbered for ready reference. They also need to be typed into an appropriately designated folder in your computer to enable copies to be printed and a master archive to be established in hard copy form. Each page needs to be suitably headed with the relevant identification for speedy retrieval. The use of a tape-recorder in some circumstances may be invaluable, but carries with it some potential dangers that must be borne in mind.

So now you are about to start collecting your data. Crucially, this means recoding your information in such a form that it is both readily accessible and readily usable. This entails not only making a note of the nature of the data but such information as the source, the date and time when it was collected and the location. Nothing is more certain than that six months after you have collected some particular data, you will have forgotten every word as to the when, where, why and how. Good record – keeping is therefore essential in this area of thesis work. Much of this information you will need to cite in due course as a necessary element in writing up your thesis. To be able to access this basic information in a usable form without having to search again for the required reference will be an immense saving of time. Therefore, it is vitally important that you organise and record your information in a way that makes this possible, even though this may be among the least interesting and most tedious aspects of the research process – certainly much less stimulating and glamorous than meeting and interviewing a variety of fascinating people with information of vital interest to you or even delving into long hidden archives and emerging with an important and fascinating fact that had been hidden for 80 years!

It is immensely dangerous to seek to avoid cutting down on the essential details in your notes on the basis that you will recall it and write it down as soon as you can after the important research event that led to the obtaining of the information. An assortment of poorly written notes splattered with your own personal abbreviations that you are unable to identify several weeks later will not suffice. You will not be able to transcribe them accurately and you will have largely forgotten much of the context and content.

Recording and organizing your data is therefore an essential part of the research process, and has to be allowed for in your research schedule or network plan. Furthermore, this allowance has to be fairly generous – remember what we said earlier; an hour's interview can easily mean three hours or more transcription. The recording of some kinds of information e.g. of observation of individual contacts within groups may be even more time-consuming, while coding information from questionnaires or recording scores from psychometric tests can be routinised and thus take up less time. It is worth reminding yourself constantly that an area of research activity you may not have altogether acknowledged as important will ultimately provide welcome benefits.

1. It will support your imperfect memory.
2. It will save details on the record that may otherwise be lost.
3. It will ultimately save time in the process of writing the thesis because

    (a) the required information is to hand and does not have to be searched for and

(b) it may already be in a form which can be immediately used in the thesis and may require relatively little re-writing.

In the case of questionnaires, the information is already available in a pre-arranged format, and with standardised interviews a similarly routinised format can be organised.

Unfortunately, not all research information can be obtained and recorded in a standardised and routine way. Suppose, for example, you are researching a biography of a long-deceased orchestral conductor or actor. You would, of course, look at any personal papers they had left to which access could be obtained, any books or articles which had been previously written about them, or newspaper or magazine items that mentioned them in some significant way.

You will undoubtedly find gaps in your information that you will need to try to fill by obtaining information from those who knew the individual in one capacity or another e.g. former colleagues, or you may find contradictory information that needs to be resolved by consulting those who might possess further details e.g. family relatives. While, if you are covering the same ground with various individuals, you might use some form of standardised aide-memoire or semi-structured format to ensure you cover the ground you needed to traverse, the respondents will almost certainly come at the questions, or indeed the whole topic, from their own particular perspective which may be a complete surprise to you, and which will not be amenable to standardisation, especially if they bring in new dimensions or facts of which you were previously completely unaware. What you can do is to seek to establish a method of organised recording that will cover a wide range of situations and sources, whether these are literature-based, interviews or observations.

Assume that you are going to conduct an interview with an elderly former colleague of the individual in whose history you are interested, because you hope the respondent can give you vital information about an issue that remains obscure in the records – perhaps the marital breakdown and divorce of the personality in question and what happened thereafter to his wife, or some period in his employment history which is not well covered in the records. There may be elements in the story that remain unclear even after an exhaustive search of the archives, and your only hope is that some information may be obtained from those who knew him at this time. After the usual preliminaries you begin the interview with an introductory question "I understand from so and so that you knew Mr X very well in the years A to B, and I wondered whether you can tell me anything about the personal circumstances of his life at this time?"

Assuming for the present that permission to use a tape recorder has been denied (and we will return to this later), then you will take rough notes in as detailed a manner as you can as the interview proceeds. These will have to be used to provide an accurate and detailed account of the information provided in the interview. This information will need to be readily retrievable and in a form you can use as required. It is assumed for the purposes of the present discussion that you will be using your personal computer to record and organise the data.

You will need to record all your notes of interviews, observations etc in a standardised form of notebook, whether of the hardbound variety or the school exercise book kind (probably depending on the number likely to be required and the expense as against the funds available), using the right hand page of the book only so that you are free to detach pages as necessary without removing potentially important information which has been written on the reverse side and may thus disappear from view. You should designate each notebook you use with a letter or number – preferably Roman numerals, particularly if you are likely to use a large number of notebooks, as there are only 26 letters in the alphabet! Each page in each notebook should then be numbered in Arabic sequence, so that you can readily refer to (notebook) III (page) 5 as III/5 etc and thus readily identify and access the origin of the information in your notes.

You will then need to add to your notes of the actual conversation in the interview any facts, information or details relating to the circumstances or situation of the interview. These notes might include observations on any or all of the following as appropriate.

- How did you come to obtain the interview?
- Who suggested the name of this respondent or provided an introduction?
- What is their relationship to or with the respondent? (This may prove to be very important, as it may have determined whether the interview process was facilitated or hindered. If your informant is in good standing with the respondent perhaps a personal friend or colleague, then your meeting is more likely to go well and the respondent may be pre-disposed to discuss the matter freely and, of course, vice versa. The problem is that you may not be aware of the situation which prevails at the time of the interview or at least, at its beginning).
- How did you come to arrange the interview – letter, telephone call or through a mutual acquaintance? All of this information is prone to be forgotten if not meticulously recorded and it may sometimes be important in providing a clue as to why you got the particular kind of response you did.
- What were the physical circumstances?
- Where did you sit?
- Where did the respondent sit?
- Was the meeting in his/her office or your office? In the sitting room at his/her home or yours? In the library at the respondent's club?
- What were the furnishings in the room?
- How was it lit?
- Did your relative physical positions change during the course of the discussion?
- Did the respondent walk about?
- Were there any interruptions? Of what kind and for how long?
- What do you know about the respondent?

- What employments, offices or posts have they held? In each case, how long did they hold these positions?
- How did they come to be involved with the subject of your discussion?
- What was the relationship? For how long?

In fact, make a note of any information you may have about the respondent that was not acquired during the course of your discussion. Some of this information may, of course, be at odds with what you are told during the course of the interview which may itself spark off further investigation or raise points of discussion in your thesis.

> Make a note of any factor that may possibly have influenced what you wrote down in your notes and its quality as evidence. Did the respondent appear embarrassed by some aspects of the conversation? Was something apparently inhibiting their response? Was the respondent over-eager to make a point? Did you feel a personal involvement with the discussion that may have affected the objectivity of your note taking? Were you able to make notes freely during the discussion? Were you able to keep up with the note taking while moving the conversation forward? How much and what did you subsequently have to write up from memory? How soon after the meeting? All of these things may impact upon the quality of the evidence you take away from the interview and subsequently influence the degree of reliance you can place upon it and the use you are able to make of it.

In order to ensure all this information can be easily retrieved and used when you need to you should type it into an appropriately named folder or file on you personal computer. This will enable you to print off however many copies you may subsequently need.

At the top of every page you will need to designate the subject of the interview, the interviewee, and the place and date of the interview so that when subsequently printed off and used for analytical purposes, any and every sheet can be readily identified and you do not have to spend valuable time trying to locate where it originally came from. You will also need to number each page, using whatever system of numeration seems most appropriate for your purposes. You may wish to number all the pages consecutively straight through your typed notes, or you may wish to relate it to the numbering system you have used in your notebooks as suggested previously e.g. III/5, or you may begin enumeration afresh at 1 for each folder or file you use.

Begin your transfer of information from each notebook to your file/folder with the data relating to the circumstances and background, the description of the setting, the information you have on the respondent derived from outside the meeting, and the notes you have made on anything affecting the quality of your data from this interview. It may also be useful as you type up the notes from the interview to indicate at the head of the page the topic being discussed at that point, so you get an impression of the flow of topics sequentially as the interview proceeded. The head of each page may therefore look something like this.

1. Subject of interview   Topic
2. Interviewee's name
3. Place of interview
4. Date of interview

From our original example of researching towards a biography of a famous orchestral conductor, the head of a page might typically look like this.

1. X's association with   Assessment of X's
  Devontown   standing as a
                conductor
2. Reg Smiley
3. The interviewee's sitting room at 7, Avondale, Devontown
4. 29 November 2007 1400–1700

The background to the meeting might appear like this.

The meeting had been arranged through the Honorary Curator of the local museum who had shown me some archival material relating to the association of the conductor with the town. I had asked if anyone in the town would now remember him and he suggested that Mr Smiley, a noted local amateur musician who had conducted the local youth orchestra for many years, had mentioned meeting the conductor.

The section relating to the physical circumstances of the interview might read something like this.

I met with Mr Smiley in the sitting room of his bungalow home in a development reserved for the elderly. He sat in an armchair on one side of the fireplace. I sat on a sofa facing the fireplace at ninety degrees from Mr Smiley's chair. There was a dining table with chairs, a bookcase and a reading desk with a radio/CD player upon it, another small desk in another corner with a personal computer on it, and a television in the corner of the room. The room itself was fitted with wall-to-wall carpets and a window that looked out over a small front garden and the road and small green opposite. There were photographs on the wall of Mr Smiley involved in various musical activities, including one large photograph of Mr Smiley himself at the head of his local amateur youth orchestra taken in the course of a concert he had presented in London ten years previously. Initially, the room was lit naturally via the window but as the winter's afternoon progressed a ceiling light and a lamp stand in the corner were switched on.

The background information on the participant might look something like this.

Mr Smiley is now in his eighties. He had pursued employment all his working life as a skilled artisan, undertaking coachwork on motorcars, pursuing his interests as a violinist and musician as a hobby in his spare time. He had met the famous conductor in the 1930s while playing in a local amateur orchestra.

The quality of the data may have been affected by a number of interruptions.

After an hour a workman known personally to Mr Smiley came to repair the back door, which gave rise to some conversation between Mr Smiley, initially his wife, and then the workman. After an hour and a half Mrs Smiley came in and positioned herself at the personal computer and spent the rest of the interview working at the computer 'on her Christmas card list' which occasioned remarks from time to time between her and her husband. At five o'clock she effectively brought the interview to an end by announcing her intention of getting her husband's tea, initiating a discussion about what this should be. It is possible she had been policing the interview with the intent of saving her husband from too difficult or strenuous a time. On several occasions she intervened in the interview with information or observations of her own and on other occasions was appealed to by her husband to refresh his memory. Half an hour before the end of the interview the arrival of Mr Smiley's daughter again occasioned an interruption. She did not share his musical interests and tastes and her presence promoted a lively but good-humoured debate between her and her father about the merits of different kinds of music and of non-musical hobbies.

When you have completed transcribing the notes of the interview you can complete the headings on each sheet. Numbers 2, 3 and 4 on each sheet would simply be

2. Mr Reg Smiley
3. Devontown
4. 29 November 2001

For number 1, if the interview dwells on the same topic for some time, you may find that the substance of a number of sheets relates to the same subject, and this will appear at the head of each sheet. In the above example, the first topic discussed may have been the background of musical activity in Devontown. Thus, the heading for these pages under topic might read 'Music in Devontown'. This might be followed by several pages, which recount the factual detail of Mr Smiley's first meeting with the conductor. The heading here then might be '*First meeting with x*'. In some cases you may have three or four topics on a page. For example, *Mr Smiley might have briefly mentioned the relationship between our conductor 'X' and conductors 'A', 'B', and 'C'*. If comments on these relationships spread over several pages in perhaps a fragmentary and mixed – up way then these headings will have to be repeated on each of these pages. This approach of using these headings may appear cumbersome at first, but in due course you will find you use it automatically and may simply record the information for these four points straight onto your personal computer without bothering to put them in your notebook.

Having completed your transcription of the interview in the above manner, you need to print out an archive copy of the finished document to serve as an 'original' hard copy as well as saving it on your personal computer and to disk. If you do this for every research event such as an observation or an interview then eventually you will have in your archive a compete set of 'originals' to which you can immediately refer should it be necessary (as it almost certainly will be) to check some point.

You will then need to print out sufficient copies of each page of the transcript to enable you to work individually with each separate topic. Fortunately, with the modern personal computer you can do this as required rather than having to depend on estimating the number of carbon copies required from typing or writing out the transcript. In the example above, let us assume that we have identified eight topics from the interview – perhaps music in Devontown; first meeting with A; relationship with 'X'; relationship with 'Y'; relationship with 'Z'; the subsequent meeting with 'A'; experience of playing under 'A'; assessment of 'A' as a conductor. The first topic is '*Music in Devontown*' so you need to print off a copy of all the pages which include the heading '*Music in Devontown*'. Some of these pages may be consecutive, some may contain the topic on pages which also contain other topics, some such pages may appear haphazardly at various points in the transcript as the respondent recalled something anew, perhaps prompted by some memory arising from the discussion, or by his wife when she became effectively a party to the interview. All of these pages containing the topic heading '*Music in Devontown*' can then be placed in a document wallet that is then appropriately labelled with the topic and the name R. Smiley. Your second topic might be '*First meeting with A*' and this needs to be treated in the same way so that you end up with a document wallet labelled R. Smiley 'First meeting with A' and containing all those pages with this topic heading included either by itself or amongst others. You then treat the remaining six topics in identical fashion, so that ultimately you have eight document wallets labelled R. Smiley with the topic clearly indicated. Clearly, for those with the requisite computer skills and a preference for reading material on screen, it may be perfectly possible to copy the material into appropriately labelled folders or files on your personal computer provided you remember to retain the necessary numerical identifiers relating to notebooks and pages. Others prefer to retain manual control and to use hard copy.

Ideally, you should try to limit the number of topics on a page, and while it is perfectly easy to carry over writing about a particular topic from one page to the next without affecting the way you use your filing system adversely – it simply means an additional sheet to print off – you might try to avoid wherever possible carrying over one line or less on the particular topic if it is going to be immediately succeeded by another topic. This makes for both less possibility of confusion and less use of paper!

One advantage of using some method of note taking such as the above is that you can use much the same system for making notes from books, journals and documents. In this case you need amend your headings at the top of the page only slightly.

1. Topic(s)
2. Reference in Harvard format: name of author; date of publication (in brackets); title of book or journal

(underlined); title of journal article; journal volume number; journal part; page range in journal; publisher of book; place of publication.

3. Location of reference – which library or libraries, website, office, museum or archive. You may wish to refer to the material again and being able to locate it easily can save an enormous amount of time.

4. Date on which you accessed the material. If the note – taking extends over a considerable period, there may be numerous dates for one reference.

Bear in mind that judicious use of photocopying material can be helpful in reducing the length of time spent on taking notes, observing, of course, any relevant copyright rules, and that if a page in the book or document covers several topics in your filing arrangements, then you may need several photocopies of the same page.

Ultimately, you will have a complete set of first copies with the sheets stapled together for each research event or session of note – taking, and a set of document wallets containing your notes allocated according to topic. These files can be checked at intervals in order to ensure that the data you are obtaining is, in fact, the information required to address the topic areas and the research question in your research proposal. As your research progresses, of course, you may find that what is emerging from your data does not match the expectations you had anticipated when drawing up the research proposal. It may be that new information has become available that is now turning the research in some different direction or has perhaps changed focus somewhat as your original assumptions are called into question or even rejected, so that some of the topics in your document wallets may no longer be relevant and new topics and document wallets will have to be added in order to reflect the new direction. The order of the files can then be arranged to match the requirements of the research proposal. You can then examine the contents of the first document wallet relating to the first topic in your research proposal, and produce an analysis and/or summary on which to base the writing up of this initial area. It may sometimes be necessary to bring together some of the points in your research proposal, but this makes no difference to the principle of the process.

It should be noted that the outline which you use for writing up your doctoral thesis, which will correspond to the order in which you place your document wallets of topics, will not necessarily be the same as that which you included in your research proposal, as this was intended to provide you with guidance relating to the data you needed to collect. Although the two may coincide, it is more likely they will not as the process of pursuing research and collecting the data will have changed your perceptions of the course of the research pathway.

While you are putting into practice the methods of recording data and sorting the material into topics preparatory for analysis as discussed here, you will, of course, work out variations which suit your particular style or mode of working and the requirements of the subject area in which you are researching. What is important is that any variations you choose to employ become part of a routine of data recording and sorting that you use consistently throughout your doctoral research work.

So far, it has been assumed that the use of a tape recorder was not possible for some reason. If it is, then this enables you to obtain an exact record of the actual words – or other audible phenomena such as music or the sounds of work being done.

Tape recording is also an asset as it means:

1. you can maintain the flow of the conversation without having to disrupt this by finding it necessary to pay attention to what you are writing;
2. it enables you to undertake some other activity in the course of the interview or other event e.g. present any necessary stimuli such as a photograph or document;

3. you may use the tape recorder to provide your own running commentary on whatever is happening.

In effect, a tape used in a tape recorder can replace the notebook stage of recording the data that was discussed earlier. It is still necessary for you to transcribe the data, print off the hard copy with the appropriate headings for each sheet and then print off the required copies to sort into the appropriate document wallets or to allocate the data, duly identified by the relevant number coding, into the folders and files you have established on your personal computer before saving these to disk once again.

There are a number of points to be borne in mind when contemplating using a tape recorder for obtaining your data.

1. Some people – whatever their reasons – will not agree to the use of a tape recorder and their wishes must be entirely respected. Any clandestine use of a tape recorder to secure your data is totally unethical and wholly unacceptable. Any use of a tape recorder must be by permission of the relevant respondent, and any request for confidentiality must be fully respected. In this regard there is no difference between material contained on your tape and material contained in your notes.

2. Bear in mind that making a written record of your interview or focus group etc and making a tape recording may give you entirely different results in terms of the way data is presented to you and how readily it is offered. You may have to make fine judgments about which technique is likely to provide you with the most fruitful rich data in a particular situation.

3. Remember that using a tape recorder to secure a record of the information a respondent provides will omit some potentially very important supporting data that can influence the interpretation that might be placed upon particular verbal responses or initiatives. Body language, facial expressions, hand gestures and head movements may all contain a wealth of meaning which can change the import and significance of a sentence. You may therefore

still need to make a note of these points to support your recordings. Equally, of course, written notes cannot capture such important features as the inflexion of a voice which again, may change the meaning that can be placed upon a sentence or remark.

4. Transcription of the tapes must take place together with any necessary editing just as soon as possible after the recorded research event has taken place. Delay here can be fatal. Vital details will be forgotten very quickly after the event, and the confusion of particular features of the event will begin to occur very soon afterwards.

5. In the very short term, you may attempt to deal with the information required to satisfy points 3 and 4 above by adding it to your tape immediately after the interview, group meeting etc However, this carries with it the danger that you will allow numerous tapes to accumulate without getting round to transcribing them. It is easy to postpone this operation under the pressure or allure of more pressing or interesting research activities. This in turn may lead to a lack of information on two very important aspects of your research progress.

   (a) Do you need to acquire further data in some particular areas of your research? Are you perhaps missing vital details on some topics?

   (b) Without altogether realizing it, have you perhaps omitted some aspects from your research possibly putting off pursuing areas of potential difficulty for the time being, until eventually you have all but forgotten about them?

6. Make sure when you set out that you are familiar with the mechanics of the machine. It has not been unknown for researchers working with a tape recorder with which they had not familiarised themselves to find out at the end of a research event that they had recorded nothing – the wrong button had been pressed or indeed no button at all. Equally, you should never go out with a tape recorder without ensuring that you have an ample supply of the correct tapes; remember that tapes come in various lengths

and that shorter lengths of tape are often easier to deal with in terms of locating a particular section you wish to replay, but for longer research events you will not wish to keep changing tapes. You should also be remember that tapes can prove faulty and can break (which is also true of tape recorders themselves – do you have a back–up to hand?) If using batteries rather than running the machine from mains electricity then it is also necessary to carry a supply of spare batteries.

When you do eventually attempt to transcribe a large volume of recorded material from your interviews, focus groups etc then the vast amount of detailed work involved can represent an almost insurmountable hurdle. You would not be the first researcher whose aspirations to submit a successful doctoral thesis have disappeared under a mountain of material that never gets transcribed!

In spite of these warnings, the tape recorder can offer an effective means of securing your data in appropriate situations. It simply needs to be borne in mind that it is not the answer to all your problems in recording data and there remain a number of potential pitfalls. Properly used, with all the attendant support activities such as prompt transcription, it represents a most valuable tool in data collection.

Most of the above points relating to audio recording apply with equal force to video recording, although the latter has not yet fully established itself as a data-recording technique to the extent that might have been anticipated given its potential.

Tutorial

Progress questions

1. Why is a good system of recording and organising data essential for the research process?
2. What information surrounding a research event of your choice e.g. an interview, focus group of non-participant observation, would you feel it necessary to record?
3. In what ways can a tape or video recording assist the collection of data?
4. What dangers may be attached to relying on tape or video recording for the collection of data?

Discussion points

1. What do you feel is the best way of recording and organising the kind of data your research is likely to collect?
2. Do you think that the use of tape and video recording is justified and is worth the possible attendant dangers and difficulties?

Practical assignments

1. Construct a draft recording system with the necessary notebook and page reference numbers to suit the methods of collection and the type of data you are likely to pursue.
2. Conduct some practice interviews or other relevant research event and transcribe the information into your record system, completing the heading on each sheet appropriately.

Study tips and revision

1. Practice putting information into your recording system so that you are wholly familiar with how it should work and test it for the research events that are likely to be involved.
2. Practice conducting interviews or other relevant research events using the data recording methods you intend to employ.

8 **Writing**

One-minute overview

It is important to commence organised and continuous writing as soon as possible, in order to develop ideas and fluency in writing and a polished quality to your work. The use of internal prompts to write may supplement the effects of occasional external prompts and make an important contribution to the development of the thesis. In order to write on a continuous basis, you need to schedule the time for writing taking into account the necessity for other activities and for the possibility of being able to employ the time usefully. It is also important to set writing milestones for both the short and the long term, bearing in mind the eventual structure of the thesis and the likely contents of each chapter. It is also useful to consider the viva as part of the structure of the thesis, and to prepare accordingly.

Now that you have received approval for your research proposal and have begun to move towards the fieldwork phase, or have perhaps even commenced it, how do you face up to the daunting process of writing up your thesis? It is not possible to be prescriptive about this as people differ in their personalities and temperaments, and an approach considered useful and workable by one author would be rejected by another simply because they do not feel comfortable approaching the task of writing-up in this way. In one sense, there are probably as many different approaches – at least in terms of variations on possible approaches – as there are individuals undertaking the activity! It is probably safe to say, however, that not many PhD candidates actually sit down and write their thesis from beginning to end in one continuous flow – although even this has been known.

There is, however, one sense in which the writing of a thesis is a continuous activity. There is always writing of one kind or another to be done. It is only by writing that you are able to

(a) develop and test your ideas and assumptions;
(b) continuously revise your work so that the polished quality you desire becomes a reality;
(c) develop fluency in writing in the way that practice develops fluency in playing the piano.

This chapter looks at a number of issues in relation to writing the thesis namely

1. getting started
2. continuing to write
3. structuring the thesis.

One of the greatest enemies to the ultimate production of a PhD thesis is the tendency to procrastinate, and nowhere is this tendency to procrastinate in greater evidence than in the effort it takes to initially put pen to paper. There is nothing easier than to say – "I haven't yet got anything worth writing about". Yet adopting the habit of writing on a regular basis is essential to getting the job done. Sometimes the initial prompt to write may come from an external source. Your supervisor may require an initial draft of the Introduction to your thesis. It is your turn to present a paper at your regular research seminar group, indicating your initial thoughts on your choice of topics, or how you are going to pursue your research in terms of methodology, or what you have discovered in undertaking your Literature Review. The problem with such external prompts as these is that they tend to be intermittent and do not necessarily result in the cultivation of the essential habit of regular writing that the production of a PhD thesis tends to require. The alternative or complementary strategy that needs to be adopted is to ensure that you provide yourself with internal prompts that will ultimately instil into you the habit of regular or daily writing that will become part of your everyday routine.

How can you find these internal prompts to write? There are numerous occasions that will present themselves in the course of your early work. It is very important that you take these early opportunities – it is both pointless and dangerous to postpone the activity until the time seems more propitious, perhaps because your review of the literature has widened and deepened your knowledge. Waiting until you have something that you feel is sufficiently significant to write about will only put you in a situation where you have to write under greater pressure, at a later date, when you will not necessarily feel any more inclined to write than you did earlier. You may conclude that there is not necessarily going to be a good time to start writing so it is better to get into the habit of doing it as early as possible!

It is important that you do not attempt to write ahead of the stage in the research process that you have actually reached. This will only cause you frustration and potentially depression, as you will be unable to articulate the things you feel you ought to be saying when in reality you are in no position to do so. This cannot contribute to the development of your ideas or provide you with any sense of progress and so may simply dampen your enthusiasm for both the research and writing. For example, in the beginning you do not necessarily need to write about the research questions or the research methods or anything as precise as this when you are unlikely to be able to do this with any degree of certainty. Rather, you can write in tentative terms, discussing various ideas about what your research might focus on or weighing in hypothetical terms the likely merits or demerits of different research methodologies or means of data collection. You might make various attempts at completing the sentence "I want to find out about..." refining your thoughts on each possibility as you go along. You can at various points move on to write about what you consider to be the next stage in the research. If you have reached the point where you have defined your research question, you might consider writing a brief but focused paper on how you see your doctorate as contributing to knowledge – what is its original contribution going to be? In what way or in what sense is it original? This, after all, is the very essence of what the doctorate is all about so it can hardly be inconsequential. If you have nothing more immediate or engaging to write about, you can write a summary for yourself of how your research has progressed since you last wrote such a summary – something you might do every week or month as the opportunity occurs. It does not necessarily have to be done in some time set aside for the purpose but perhaps while sitting over an extra cup of coffee in the evening. This is a very useful exercise to undertake at reasonably regular intervals. It may bring to your attention gaps in your progress that you had overlooked, things you had forgotten to do or had not realised had become more urgent and important as events had unfolded or which you had merely continuously put off doing because you found them difficult or in some way unattractive or potentially unpleasant to do. Again, you might have come across a problem you need to address in the course of your work and writing a paper on the subject may help you clarify the issues and the possible alternative solutions. One aspect of this is that you might write about concepts, theories and models that might be useful in connection with your research even if only in terms of providing background understanding. You may never need to actually use these papers in the thesis itself but they can help to provide understanding and insight into related ideas and concepts which may be relevant, for example by providing you with a history of the development of a particular debate, especially in subject areas where you may never previously have studied.

Writing in this manner may make a number of important contributions to the development of your work.

1. It provides important practice in writing and in acquiring the habit of writing.
2. It builds your confidence that you can actually write a major thesis.
3. It provides a source of ideas that you can use or develop if they seem useful perhaps at a later stage, also allowing you to reject ideas that do not seem likely to prove useful.
4. It may provide a source of quotations, sentences, references, ways of saying things that seem particularly apposite and can ultimately be transferred effectively to the thesis itself.

5. It may enable you to engage in discussion with your supervisor or fellow researchers on the basis that you are developing your thinking and that what you have written is in no way definitive even as a draft.

To enable yourself to write on a continuous basis there are a number of things you need to consider and make allowance for meeting.

1. Schedule the times when you are going to write. You may try to make this the same period of the day as far as possible, which has the merit of building it into your daily routine and time management process. Even when this is not possible, you still need to allocate time ahead on your research schedule to ensure that this crucial activity does not get postponed indefinitely. In scheduling times you need to

   (a) take account of other things you need to do e.g. paid employment, family time, social activities and friends, holidays or travel time

   (b) be realistic in estimating how much time you have left and how you can use it

   (c) bear in mind the need for activities surrounding writing, including revision and editing

   (d) prioritise your writing, the need for which may become clearer as you progress and this may require you to provide longer or more frequent writing slots than you were using previously.

2. Make sure the time allocated is such that it can be employed usefully. It has to be time when:

   (a) there are unlikely to be interruptions or you can take steps to exclude them e.g. the telephone, or family

   (b) you can apply yourself continuously over a substantial period of time. Short blocks of time e.g. between holding classes or on short railway journeys can be usefully employed on activities related to writing such as revising previously written texts for errors in sentence construction, punctuation or grammar, recording ideas or references, but not for extensive new writing.

3. Time is needed for activities surrounding both ends of a writing session.

   (a) In the beginning you need to look through what you wrote in the last session of writing and examine the notes you may have prepared for use in the current session so that you begin writing with a clear idea of the context in which you are writing and the direction in which you are going.

   (b) At the end of the session you need to round off the session by making sure you have identified clearly the point at which you will commence next time, perhaps by making a note in the text on your personal computer or even an outline in note form of the next paragraph or passage of text to move you quickly and smoothly into the next session of writing. You may also here identify any references, points or arguments, data or previously rehearsed and especially apt sentences or phrases you intend to use, in order to ensure you do not pass over these when your memory may have faded by the next day or the next week.

How much you write and when and how often you write tends to be a matter of personal preference and how your time is structured. Some people will write 500 or 1,000 words a day of whatever kind or for whatever purpose. After all, assuming that your thesis will be somewhere in the region of 75,000 words, then at only 500 words a day you would complete a draft of the submission in five months, although of course it would not be as simple as that. Others will operate more in terms of allocating so much time a day or week, building this into the way they manage their time each day or each week, or even each month, although this may be taking too long a perspective. Much depends on whether you are someone who prefers to write in relatively small bites of perhaps 500–1000 words a time bearing in mind the fragmentation of style this may bring with it if you are not careful and which may need extensive revision eventually, or whether you prefer to write in longer spells with wider intervals between writing sessions, when it may take a little time to get back into the frame of mind in which you were writing and to pick up from the point you had reached.

What is essential is that whichever approach you adopt, you set yourself writing milestones – both short term – what is to be achieved by the end of next week or next month, or at the end of three months – and long term ones – what is to be achieved by certain dates next year, which inevitably will be rather more flexible.

When you commence writing it is helpful to bear in mind the eventual structure of the thesis. Most theses have a broad structure in common, although inevitably there are variations where the nature of the discipline involved or perhaps the nature and discussion of the data presented or results obtained demand it. A typical structure might look something like this.

1. Abstract
2. Introduction
3. Literature Review
4. Contextual Background
5. Research Methods
6. Results
7. Analysis and Discussion of Results
8. Conclusions
9. References
10. Appendices

Most theses usually contain an abstract bound into the front of the submission. In some cases, institutions may require further loose copies of the abstract to be submitted, perhaps three, for examination purposes. Abstracts constitute a very important part of the thesis on two counts:

1. they provide an overview in succinct form of a lengthy and detailed research study
2. they enable those who might be interested to decide whether the thesis is of sufficient concern to them as to be worth reading.

Normally, an abstract will contain an outline of the following matters.

1. The purpose and context of the research.
2. The hypotheses, which were tested, or the research questions which the thesis attempts to answer.
3. What the sample(s) or subjects were.
4. The research methods used.
5. The principal conclusions.
6. The importance and relevance of the thesis to the field of study.

While the above list may seem straightforward, reducing perhaps 80,000 or even more words to a mere 300 (or whatever length of abstract your institution requires) is a formidable proposition and often requires many attempts before the desired length is attained while retaining the essential aspects of the above elements. It is, nevertheless, essential, and the abstract may subsequently be placed in one or more of the various indexes of theses that are available. It is also worth noting that practice in abstract writing can be very useful, as many journals require these as a form of introduction to any articles they use for publication.

The ability to write a cogent and lucid abstract may be taken as an indication of the mastery of the contents of the study by the PhD candidate who through the medium of a brief synopsis can demonstrate the nature and scope of the work, the significant results, and how the research makes its original contribution to the study of the field in question. You should always read carefully the requirements laid down by your particular institution for the submission of the abstract of theses. Is it 300 words maximum that is required or some other figure? Is it to be single or double-spaced? If you are required to submit a number of loose copies of the abstract you will need to ensure that your name, the title of the thesis and the year of submission are all included below the heading ABSTRACT, and you may be required to submit this information in capital letters. All of this detail needs to be checked and attended to.

Following the Abstract the first piece of substantial writing is the Introduction. It is often worth drafting an initial Introduction very soon after you have begun to make decisions about the precise topic you are going to pursue and how you are going to pursue it. At this stage, of course, you will have no idea of what the results of your research are going to be or their possible significance so you cannot refer to these things, but you can begin to draft a response to the various questions that need to find a response in the Introduction. These questions include the following.

1. What is the hypothesis, which has been tested, or the research question that has been answered?
2. Why is it interesting and important?
3. What original contribution does it make to the field of study?
4. How and why did you become interested in it?
5. Why and how was the research conducted?
6. What have been the significant elements in the findings?
7. How can the results be used? For example, has it led to the identification of the need for further research, perhaps in different directions?

All of this is presented in a brief and succinct style as many of these questions will be dealt with in much greater depth in the body of the text.

The Introduction is a very important element in the thesis. It is here that you set out your stall and say to potential readers – including examiners – 'look, I have something very interesting to say here'. It is also important to realise that just as research is very often an iterative process, so the Introduction may need to be re-visited and re-written many times during the course of your work – indeed it may well be the first and the last thing you write (with the possible exception of the Abstract). As your perspectives on the research change so will your approach, as reflected in the Introduction.

The initial writing of the Introduction often serves wonderfully well to force upon you the need to clarify your thinking about a number of important aspects of your research and the re-writing process likewise forces you to review in a focused and critical way the changes you have made or are proposing to make to the research and how it is conducted.

Literature Reviews make a major contribution to any thesis, and may be regarded as central to your thesis. They fulfil a number of purposes.

1. To demonstrate that you have read extensively in your chosen area of research.
2. To show your ability to critically analyse and use existing theory relating to your research question(s).
3. To identify the practical problem(s) that your thesis may be attempting to address.
4. To recognise the contribution other writers have made in the field.
5. To inform your own research and suggest possible modifications e.g. in refining your research question or hypothesis.

It must be emphasised that a literature review is not a list, catalogue or survey. It is a means of enabling you (and others who read your work) to understand in a structured way the research question or problem you are addressing. What is not required is

> "uncritical catalogues of all that has been found which vaguely relates to the topic regardless of the merits of the work" (Gill and Johnson, 1997:21).

What is required, therefore, is a critical analysis or review not a descriptive account of what others have written.

1. There is a tendency for some researchers to become enmeshed in the task of reading vast quantities of literature with two possible consequences:

   (a) it becomes a means of procrastination to avoid the difficult and taxing task of actually writing something;

(b) it does not necessarily assist in the process of developing original ideas as the researcher becomes overwhelmed by the ideas of other writers.

"Accordingly, the state of the literature search needs to be kept under close review, in consultation with supervisors and colleagues, to avoid becoming over concerned with other people's work at the expense of creativity" (Gill and Johnson, 1997:21).

2. There is a need to avoid merely providing as uncritical catalogue of everything you have found which is somehow vaguely related to your research question – a defect that is disappointingly present all too frequently in many theses. As Gill and Johnson put it,

"What is required is an insightful evaluation of what is known which leads naturally to an identification of the gaps in the field and the way in which the proposed research is intended to fill them."

3. The researcher often omits to make a systematic note of everything that is read at the time. The danger is that even after a very short time, memory fades and becomes indistinct, and a considerable amount of time may be lost in searching for the exact location (or indeed the exact quotation) that was not recorded at the time of reading.

In order to record such information, index cards (3x5) are still very much in use, and each source needs to be recorded in ink on one or more of these. It is helpful if you use the same format on these index or bibliographic cards as you will use later in preparing the final bibliography, as you can then simply transcribe the information on the cards into the bibliography. The information that you require to be listed on the cards is as follows.

1. Name of the author(s).
2. Title of the book or journal, and the title of the article in the journal.
3. Date and place of publication with the name of the publisher for a book.

4. For journals, in addition to the date, you should record the volume number and the part number, together with the complete page range for the article.

5. Pages that contain useful information together with a brief note indicating why this source may be useful.

6. In the top right hand corner of the card, indicate the location(s) of the source e.g. Senate House Library, University of London. If there is more than one location known to you then record them, as this may be useful as you cannot always be sure of obtaining access at one location just when you require it.

7. In the top left hand corner of the card, record the call or access number of the source, or whatever other identification mark is used, so that it can be recalled easily when required.

One of the arts you will need to develop for research purposes is that of skimming books and articles to establish the major ideas or information they contain in order to determine their usefulness as a source. If a book or article seems helpful at an initial skimming, then time can be set aside for further and more careful reading. If not, then it can be discarded in favour of more promising leads. However, it is useful to retain for reference purposes the index card you created for the source. It may later prove to be more valuable and relevant than you originally thought, and if so, it will be helpful to be able to return to it with ease.

It has already been said that what is needed in a literature review is critical analysis of the published work included not merely reproduction in a descriptive way of what others have said. Many researchers find this difficult initially, and often ask how a critical review can be approached. It must be emphasised that the term critical review used in this context does not mean making unpleasant remarks about the books or papers under consideration. The term critical review or critical analysis means rather 'evaluation and interpretation'. There are these two aspects to the task – you may interpret a work without necessarily overtly evaluating it and you may evaluate a work without explicitly interpreting it. For many works you read for your research purposes, you will need to do both. Critical analysis also necessarily involves your perspective. What is it that you are looking for? What you may find in a book or paper may depend on what you are looking for.

In terms of evaluation, it is clear that some sources are worth more than others with regard to their level of scholarship, the skill with which the argument is developed, and the accuracy of the evidence used. It is often a difficult task to distinguish between what is worthwhile and what is not among the writings of acknowledged authorities in the field. As Winkler and McCuen (1979) indicate, there are some guidelines that can be used for evaluating the varying quality of the different sources available.

1. Always use the most recent source that you can find on the basis that the opinion found there is more likely to reflect current views. Always use the later of two sources if they differ only in date.

2. All assertions made by one source – whether controversial or commonplace – should always be tested and verified by the views of others. Academic debate involves writers discussing and commenting upon the work of peers and colleagues – and themselves in turn finding their work being discussed and commented upon. It becomes possible after reading in a number of sources to make a judgement about the current consensus of opinion amongst the acknowledged authorities, or about the rival camps into which they have divided themselves, and what the reputation of a particular academic or writer is – although the dissenting voice may ultimately be vindicated and shown to be correct, and the maverick may serve the function of stimulating debate.

3. You yourself should evaluate the evidence and logic of any source you intend to use. While this may appear difficult, it principally requires common sense and attention to detail in order to establish whether a particular source is convincing or whether there are unexplained inconsistencies in the evidence provided, assumptions whose presence is

never justified or leaps in the argument which are not supported by evidence or where the evidence is capable of providing other explanations.

4. Critical reviews in academic and professional journals may provide an indication of how others working in the particular field have themselves evaluated the work. While the personal perspectives and prejudices of the reviewer may often become apparent, probably in the course of a hostile review which may itself cause you to question the reviewer's judgement and evaluation, nevertheless, some useful points may be made about the strengths and weaknesses of a contribution made by a certain researcher in the relevant field.

From a practical standpoint, critical analysis of what you are reading can be conducted by posing a series of questions to yourself about the work.

1. Who is saying this?
2. Why are they saying it?
3. What is the basis on which they are saying it?
4. Is this basis sound?
5. What is the particular perspective from which the subject is approached?
6. What have others said about this work?
7. How does what it says relate to your research question or problem?

As Swetnam (1997) puts it:

"Your main problem will be to balance correctly the use of quotation from the work of others with critical gloss and evaluative comment of your own. A common fault of literature reviews is to sprinkle references liberally around with insufficient thought as to how they fit in to the theory and the theme. Every time a work is referred to or a quotation included apply the mental test 'So what?' In other words what is this reference adding to the development of my theory; how does it follow the thread of the dissertation and how does it relate to my research questions?

When transferring your notes on the literature into the actual literature review, check the reasons why each reference will illuminate or complement your work." *(Swetnam, 1997:61–62)*

He goes on to suggest that one or more of the following must apply in each case.

1. It deals with theory that underpins your work.
2. It makes a definitive statement about an aspect of your study.
3. It deals with your subject area or overlaps it.
4. It shows your acknowledgement of the work of others.
5. It assists in the maintenance of a coherent argument.
6. It puts your work into an external context.
7. It defines the current state of research in your area.

The Contextual Background (or something of similar intent if not the exact title) is a chapter that does not necessarily appear in all PhD theses or in suggested structures for such theses. This is because sometimes the relevant information can be found in the Introduction, the Literature Review, the Research Methods and even the Analysis and Discussion of the Results whether in one of these chapters or in combination. Nevertheless, it is a useful chapter to keep in the framework of your structure until such time as you definitely decide to dispense with it on the basis that the information is better placed and presented elsewhere in the thesis.

The purpose of the chapter or its equivalent is to provide a survey of some of the antecedents of the research. This may involve presenting the historical background starting in a fairly broad way and then focusing down increasingly tightly towards the event or organisation on which the research question at the heart of your thesis is centred. The reason that this chapter (or its equivalent) is essential is that you cannot assume that the reader – even an examiner – is necessarily sufficiently conversant with the history of the context or with all aspects of the context in which the research took place, to be able to place the locus of the research question in that context.

For example, you might be looking at the economic forces that drove the latest manifestation of merger and acquisition activity in the supermarket retailing industry in the United Kingdom. Such mergers and acquisitions may have been commonplace in the industry since it developed in the early 1960s, and as a consequence many once famous names have disappeared from British high streets. Your reader or examiner may well be an expert on the economics of oligopoly market structures or on the retail distribution of food products or the financing of mergers and takeovers, but may not be aware of the background economic history leading up to the latest developments in mergers and acquisitions in this area of retailing. A contextual account which provided a sense of the history of the introduction of supermarket retailing into the United Kingdom and of how competition between the various chains which were initially established led to mergers and acquisitions and to the strategic development of existing chains of grocery stores, focusing down towards the evolution of the current oligopoly market which is carefully scrutinised by the Office of Fair Trading would serve to place your research in its historical context for the benefit of the reader who may not be so well informed upon the subject.

Similarly, you might have pursued a research project on the administration of secondary schools in Scotland. A brief overview of the history of secondary schools in Scotland and their administration with a developing focus on the growth of the concept of the professionalisation of public sector management generally and how this came to be developed in Scottish secondary schools before arriving at a discussion of the management of your subject schools would be helpful to a reader – including perhaps an examiner from an English university – who was unfamiliar with the distinctive history, philosophy and structure of secondary school education in Scotland.

The same might be said of a study of a structural reorganisation within the National Health Service in England, where a broad account of the introduction and development of the National Health Service in England, the factors in, for example, technology and epidemiology which have influenced the structural changes which have been attempted, leading up to your account of the latest organisational change which is the subject of your study, and how it fits in with what has gone before, might provide important contextual insights for the reader.

You should never assume that readers of your thesis, including examiners, have the same knowledge and command of the contextual background that your studies have given to you.

The Research Methods chapter provides an account of the way the research process has been structured and the research methods employed. It provides an indication of the research paradigm involved which will reflect your basic beliefs about the world and determine the research design you are likely to use, how your data will be collected and analysed and "even the way in which you wrote your thesis" (Hussey and Hussey, 1997:47). As Morgan (1979) put it, the term can be used in three different ways:

1. philosophically – to reflect basic beliefs about the world
2. socially – to provide guidelines about how research should be conducted
3. technically – to specify the research methods and techniques which should be adopted.

In providing this element in the discussion of the research methods you are therefore

1. personally recognizing and understanding your personal paradigm as it has influenced the conduct of your research and
2. making this paradigm and its influence known to the reader.

The two principal paradigms are:

1. positivist – which may sometimes be described as

- quantitative
- objectivist
- scientific
- experimental
- traditionalist

2. phenomenological – which may sometimes be described as

- qualitative
- subjectivist
- humanistic
- interpretivist.

Note that the terms listed under each paradigm are not necessarily always seen as interchangeable and may be used differently by different authors in order to convey the sense of a different approach. Further, although two major paradigms are commonly cited, these may be regarded as the two ends of a spectrum, with some of the features and assumptions of one paradigm being relaxed and replaced by some from the other paradigm as you move along the spectrum (Hussey and Hussey 1997:47–48). Cresswell (1994) provides an account of the different assumptions of the two paradigms, while Hussey and Hussey (1997:46–78) provide an accessible discussion of the concepts and issues.

From the discussion of your paradigm (which will not necessarily be longer than a paragraph or so) it should be relatively easy to move seamlessly into a justification of the research methods you have chosen to use. You may have noted here the use of the term 'research methods' rather than 'research methodology'. It is now often the case that authors distinguish between these two terms.

"Methodology refers to the overall approach to the research process from the theoretical underpinning to the collection and analysis of data." In this sense it is clearly related to the paradigm you adopt.

"Methods, on the other hand, refer only to the various means by which data can be collected and/or analysed.

Thus methodology is concerned with the following main issues:

1. Why certain data was collected.
2. what data was collected.
3. from whom it was collected.
4. when it was collected.
5. how it was collected.
6. how it was analysed."
(Hussey and Hussey, 1997:54).

You will need to justify the choice of the research methods you employ and perhaps indicate, if appropriate, the reasons why other research methods were rejected or otherwise not considered. It may be, for example, because the current state of knowledge in the topic area rendered the use of a questionnaire inappropriate as it was not possible to establish with certainty the necessary questions to be asked, so some prior research would be needed to get to this point, or perhaps it was impossible to select an appropriate sample without a suitable sampling frame. It is often the case that the actual data collected and the means of collection depend upon purely practical issues. This is acceptable provided the means of data collection used is properly justified and appropriately rigorous.

In addition to the choice of data collection tools or instruments, this area of the thesis will also discuss, as appropriate,

1. the development of data collection tools and instruments e.g. questionnaires, interview schedules, experimental procedures, psychological tests;
2. the pilot tests which were undertaken in the above processes as relevant;
3. the selection of samples;
4. the time scale on which the research was implemented;
5. the means by which the collected data were analysed.

The importance of the use of pilot studies in, for example, the development of a questionnaire, interview schedule or other techniques where they are relevant cannot be over-emphasised. It is also absolutely essential that the analytical techniques applied are justified and described in detail, and in this way are available for scrutiny. Again, this is an area of the thesis (and, equally importantly, the research proposal) that is often glossed over or dismissed in few words whereas it is a vital part of the discussion of the research methods. Without appropriate analytical techniques properly applied – and seen to be properly applied – the most sophisticated data collection and analytical techniques and the most potentially interesting data are rendered futile.

It is also necessary in this chapter to consider how the research was actually implemented – in what ways and by using what methods of organisation was the research actually pursued in practice. Data collection and the associated strategies need to be organised and administered. How was this done? What steps were involved in accumulating the necessary evidence to systematically answer your research questions? These need to be fully described, as does the application of your analysis to the data and other evidence collected (Allison, 1997:31).

Finally, in the course of this discussion, it is necessary to squarely face up to any problem you experienced in this phase of your research. Few research studies escape problems in the course of their implementation e.g. being granted access to archival data only to find that the material is not held in the way you were given to understand or in a form which you can readily use or again, you found that completed questionnaires were not being returned in the numbers you had hoped or anticipated. What did you do about it? You must fully reveal these problems and the steps you took to deal with them, the justification for those steps, and how successful they were in actually resolving the difficulty. To admit to having experienced problems and having made attempts to deal with them – perhaps not altogether successfully – is not a sign of weakness but rather a sign of strength and confidence in your ability to cope with the exigencies of the research environment.

The Results chapter needs to present clearly the findings that you have established. This is more difficult to do than it may sound, and prior planning of the chapter and in particular the order in which the results are to be presented is necessary. One principle that may inform this planning is to test all the data that might conceivably be included in the chapter with the following questions.

1. How does this relate to my research question or hypothesis?
2. How does this advance the argument in the thesis?

It is always likely that you will come across data that are interesting in themselves, but which do not relate directly to your research question or hypothesis. By all means make a note of these for future reference – perhaps to be pursued at a later date – but do not include them in this chapter, whatever the temptation. The data or evidence you present will, after all, be analysed in relation to the research questions or hypothesis.

If your study is positivistic or quantitative in nature, then the facts are likely to be presented in the form of tables and figures, with an indication of their relevance and importance. Any discussion of these will normally follow in the next chapter. A position may arise where there is an extensive list of tables or figures to be presented. In this case you may have to exercise a degree of judgment as to whether to present all the tables and figures in one chapter and discuss all of these in the succeeding chapter, or whether such an approach might make the data indigestible. The issue of indigestibility might be exacerbated if the reader has to keep referring back to the required information in the tables. If you feel this might be the outcome of such an approach then it might be better, if it can be done with organisational coherence, to break the tables down into two or even three chapters relating to different aspects of the research and to present the tables or figures in separate chapters relating to each of these categories accompanied by the discussion associated with the separate categories. The threads of the discussion can then be woven together as a totality in your Conclusion or even an additional chapter of discussion, although this is probably relatively unlikely unless the discussion proves to be a lengthy one.

In the case of phenomenological or qualitative theses the position may well be more complex as the results, analysis and discussion may be effectively impossible to unravel. Instead, therefore, of separate chapters for Results and Discussion, it may be more useful if a large amount of data have been collected and/or the analysis is particularly extensive, to present the Results and Discussion combined together over two chapters. It is necessary in this case, as with the quantitative example cited above, to find some logical way of dividing the material to provide chapters that are complete and satisfying in themselves, and to ensure that however you handle the results and the discussion, the purpose of your presentations remains as being to enable the reader to make sense of the data and your interpretation.

Whether you are dealing with quantitative or qualitative data, it is this point about making sense of the data that determines how the results should be organised. There is no one single, definitive answer and in many cases a degree of flexibility will have to be used when deciding on the most helpful approach. Ultimately, there has to be

(a) a logic to the organisation of the results which readers can recognise and
(b) this logic must assist readers in finding their way through the results.

There are some simple observations that might be helpful.

1. Commence with a short statement or paragraph that tells the reader how the Results chapter is organised and provides an idea of what is in the chapter and the logic behind the organisation.
2. Do not confront the reader with a large mass of data.
3. Do not provide an extended discussion here:

   (a) the interpretation and significance of findings can be threshed out in the Discussion chapter

(b) the repetition in verbal form of the information contained in the table is unnecessary.

What the reader needs is to be taken clearly through the findings, with the points that you consider to be of particular importance flagged up for future reference later in the thesis.

Rudestam and Newton (2001) suggest three basic sections for most Results chapters.

1. The description of the sample e.g. the demographics relating to the sample, presented in written or tabular form, or variables that describe the characteristic of the unit of analysis being studied.
2. The examination of the research questions and/or testing of hypotheses.
3. The examination of additional questions generated by the previous analysis or further explanatory investigation (if these occur or are appropriate or relevant).

Try to reduce the quantity of data presented if at all possible. Some findings may be found not to be significant, and it may be possible to state this without presenting the actual data, although this cannot be done in the case of a major hypothesis.

You may well have to make judgments about how important specific findings are, and as the researcher who has examined these, it is your responsibility to decide that it may be acceptable to ignore or provide only a passing comment on what you consider to be unimportant. Never, however, confuse what is unimportant and what you may wish to ignore because it does not support your hypothesis or your assumptions contained in your research question (Rudestam and Newton, 2001:103–7).

The analysis and discussion chapter(s) should begin with a restatement of the research objective(s) and the research question(s) or hypotheses. These serve to give purpose and direction to the chapter – they are, after all, essentially what the thesis is all about.

In this chapter several objectives should be met.

1. Demonstrate the original contribution made to existing knowledge.
2. Show the significance of the results for future research.
3. Discuss any shortcomings in the research design – be self-critical and show you have learnt from experience.
4. Suggest how future studies might remedy any design deficiencies.

Rudestam and Newton (2001) have suggested some possible sections for this chapter.

1. An overview of the significant findings of the study.
2. A consideration of the findings in the light of existing research studies.
3. Implications of the study for current theory (except in purely applied studies).
4. A careful examination of findings that fail to support or only partially support your hypothesis.
5. Limitations of the study that may affect the validity or the generalisability of the results.

(Rudestam and Newton, 2001:167–8)

It is important that in the course of discussing your findings you do not make any claims that go beyond what the evidence will support. Any exaggeration or statements that are too wide-ranging or unqualified may be seized upon in the viva, particularly as the chapter is likely to be a focus of the examiners' attention. In a sense, this chapter follows on from the Introduction and the Literature Review and may reflect these in terms of what it contains and the way in which it is written. Thus, you will do the following things.

1. Use the basis of the collected data to advance the conceptual argument.
2. Explore the meaning of the data, using any relationships that emerge in the study.
3. Evaluate whether you have answered the research question – to what extent and in what ways – using your data as far as possible.

4. Consider the possibility of alternative interpretations of the data – how far does your data and the interpretations you have put upon it compare with other interpretations?
5. Place the results of the study within the theoretical context from the literature review– if appropriate considering each result in turn.
6. Cite relevant studies and the literature:

   (a) to look for new ways of interpreting and understanding the results
   (b) to provide further evidence in confirmation or otherwise of your understanding.

There are some things that should not be included in the discussion chapter:

1. a repetition of the presentation of the results: the findings should be discussed not described again;
2. a repetition and reformulation of points already made;
3. an apology for shortcomings of the study

   (a) any major design faults require a consideration of the reasons for the adoption of the design;
   (b) unintended faults or limitations to the study may reasonably be identified in evaluating the strength of the conclusions;

4. pointless meandering – stick to your focus and its logic;
5. immoderate language with which to talk up your conclusions – "whopping", "astounding", "amazing", "extraordinary" and similar words should be avoided in order to maintain a balanced and credible account.

Conclusions are often found to be very difficult to write. It is frequently the case that a poor Conclusions chapter mars otherwise sound thesis presentations so that the thesis limps weakly from the stage. Both the Introduction and the Conclusion are vital elements in attracting the attention of the reader to the thesis and in proclaiming that this is a study which has something to say and is worth reading. Their importance is such that some examiners will read the Introduction and then the Conclusion before turning to the rest of the thesis. It is surprising that some otherwise admirable books on the writing of a PhD thesis have comparatively little to say on the subject of the Conclusion.

In fact, the Introduction and the Conclusion might be said in some sense to be the reverse image of each other. The Introduction commences with a discussion of the broad context of the study and then increasingly focuses down to the actual research question or hypothesis. By contrast, the Conclusion commences with the main points of the research and then proceeds to place these within the broader context showing how the study leads to the possibility of further research in the same area and why this is important both in general terms and in advancing knowledge in this subject.

The important issues on relation to the Introduction and the Conclusion are these.

1. They need to complement each other.
2. The same key terms need to appear in both the Introduction and the Conclusion.
3. The Conclusion should show that the aims stipulated in the Introduction have been met or should contain an explanation as to why this is not the case.

Hussey and Hussey (1997) have provided a useful guide to writing what they label the summary and conclusions chapter.

- "Restate the purpose of the research.
- Summarise the main points from the results and show how they address your research questions.
- Give guidance on the implications of your research, such as who might be affected by your findings and how that will affect behaviour, attitudes and policies, etc
- Do not offer new opinions.
- Identify the weaknesses in your research and the limitations of your study.
- Suggest what future research might be conducted and how your study helps.

- In the same way that you spent quite a bit of time choosing the opening of the introductory chapter, you should spend a long time on the last sentence. Aim for a convincing ending."

(Hussey and Hussey 1997:293).

Bear in mind when writing the Conclusion that its purpose is to describe the meaning and significance of the analysis of the data in relation to the research questions or hypotheses, and your conclusions about the meaning and significance need to be made clear. The conclusions also need to be related back to the theoretical concepts and framework(s) that were cited in your Literature Review as underpinning the study, and, if appropriate, the implications of the conclusions for practice may need to be considered (Allison, 1997:31).

Bouma and Atkinson (1995:240) suggest that referring back to the statement of the research problem or hypothesis is a useful way of beginning to organise a conclusion.

Coombes (2001:200) argues that if your hypothesis is not supported or the research produces an inconclusive outcome, then the problem of writing a conclusion is exacerbated. This is because:

1. researchers, particularly inexperienced researchers, may become emotionally attached to an expected outcome for the topic;
2. nevertheless, it is essential to avoid a biased conclusion obtained from writing on the basis of your feelings;
3. the necessary impartiality is difficult to maintain.

In fact, it is important that the Conclusion addresses the outcome of your research in such a way that it is open and honest. Even if the outcomes are negative or inconclusive, ÿthere may be important issues for future research e.g. regarding the research design or the research methods employed, including the nature and size of the sample used. In these circumstances, the researcher can add to the usefulness of the findings by making a comment on some of the basic issues relating to the conduct of the research.

1. Did the research design and the research methods employed achieve the objectives of the research? If not, in what ways and to what extent did they fall short?
2. Did the sample of respondents that actually materialised differ from that originally intended? If so, in what ways and to what extent did it differ, and why?
3. What problems arose during the actual conduct of the data collection and its analysis? How were these problems dealt with? How far were these problems dealt with? How far were the solutions successful? Did weaknesses remain in the research process? If so, what were these and how important were they in terms of influencing the outcome?

Answers to questions like these may be very significant to the conduct of future research in this area and may provide an important element in the justification of what you have done in relation to actually getting your PhD in spite of negative or inconclusive outcomes.

In line with the above comments, it is important to ensure that the purposes of a conclusion are clearly understood and become the focus of your writing at this point.

These purposes are to provide:

1. a powerful and thoughtful end to what you have written;
2. a survey of what has been discovered or learnt from your research;
3. a critical evaluation of the outcomes of the research – how has it been beneficial and rewarding, and what applications it may have;
4. a way forward for future research.

As Coombes (2001:201) points out, there are a number of things that a researcher should not do in writing a good conclusion.

1. Do not just summarise what has happened.
2. Do not introduce a new idea at this point in the thesis.
3. Do not over-emphasise or focus on a minor point from the research.
4. Do not seek to cover up or gloss over any part of the work that is incomplete or contains weaknesses – always be honest.
5. Do not apologise for putting forward your view as based on the evidence you have obtained – as Coombes puts it do not say anything like 'at least this is what I believe'.
6. Do not engage in repetition.

A good Conclusion, read in conjunction with the Abstract and/or the Introduction, should make the significance of your research clear. All of these sections of your thesis should be relatively short.

It may sometimes happen that a new idea may emerge late in the research process and hence potentially late in the thesis. It can occur particularly in qualitative forms of research when the interaction between the results, analysis and discussion can produce outcomes that cause you to rethink the possible relationship between some variables or issues and to re-examine the question(s) you have asked as you come to view the research in a slightly different light. This may, in turn, lead you to focus your research in a different way and the process can become cumulative as one thing leads to another. What you need to do in this circumstance is to provide a logical summary of what has happened explaining the nature and process of what has occurred. You should not try to fit this new situation into the former configuration of the research, where it may not sit at all comfortably. You cannot honestly and effectively present what you now have into the former pattern and shape that was anticipated – the new wine may not mature appropriately in the old bottle!

There are a number of difficulties in presenting conclusions that you need to keep in mind.

1. Staying focused on the objectives of the research. These may perfectly appropriately have changed during the

course of the research. It is valid to make such changes, but your conclusions must focus on the new objectives. You will need to address briefly the nature of the changes and the reasons for them in the Conclusion. It is also important that you continue to focus on the chosen objectives of the research – whether changed or not – and not those you wish you had pursued, or which you now think might ultimately be more interesting – you cannot move the goalposts in relation to the objectives at the concluding stage however much you might wish to do so – and some PhD candidates do attempt to do this!

2. Placing the research in context i.e. moving from the specific focus of your research back to the more general area of which it is part. This is what gives your research its significance but many PhD candidates fail to do this effectively, preferring to stay with their specific focus perhaps for reasons of feeling less secure in the wider context.

3. Succumbing to the temptation to provide detailed information relating to some other part of the thesis e.g. the research methods or the analysis of the results. What is required here is a very brief account of what the research tells us, and particularly what the value of this is and what the possible implications might be.

4. Related to the above point is having a concluding chapter which is headed 'Summary and Conclusion' and then spending a great deal of time on 'Summary' (often with much repetition) and perhaps only a page or less on 'Conclusions', which suggests that the candidate has little real idea of what the term 'conclusions' actually means. This can often be a reason for referring the thesis back for rewriting.

5. Including recommendations that bear little relationship to your conclusions and findings. It is sometimes the case that institutions may even require that practical recommendations are made but these should never be invented or be unrelated to your conclusions and findings. If such recommendations are not a requirement and the outcome of your thesis does not naturally produce these then do not feel obliged to create them where they do not exist.

6. Bringing in incomplete or negative results – which can be emotionally difficult and raise feelings of insecurity. Nevertheless, these aspects of your research, if present, should be included however unsatisfactory you may feel they might be. The purposes of this are to:

(a) provide other researchers with a useful baseline from which to start work;

(b) prevent fruitless replication of what has been shown to be a blind alley or a futile approach;

(c) indicate where and how the research work might usefully be taken forward e.g. in a different area of the field of study or by using a different research method, perhaps changing the nature of the research question or the sample used.

The final element in the structure of the thesis that needs to be considered is the viva. It may seem strange to think of the viva as part of the structure of the PhD. However, in the viva you will be required to defend and justify verbally what you have written. You will have to respond to the examiners' probing on various elements in your thesis. What happens in the viva is therefore very much about your writing and what happens to it once it goes beyond the immediate circle of your supervisor, colleagues, fellow students and others who may have contributed by reading and commenting upon it at various formative stages in its production. It goes to an external examiner who is perhaps the first of a wider public who may see and evaluate the fruit of your labour.

The term viva is used here in its United Kingdom context and essentially involves a closed meeting between examiners (normally an external examiner and an internal examiner who has not been involved in the research and its supervision) and the candidate. The supervisor may be present by invitation of the examiners, but does not actually take part in the examination (although, again by invitation he or she may be involved in the discussion). Not all countries employ the style of PhD examination used in the United Kingdom where independent examining is heavily emphasised. Both the

United States and European countries employ a different style of examining involving the dissertation committee and other faculty members in the United States and in the case of European universities a public defence with members of the department and an external examiner involved and in front of a public audience. In reality, in the case of the United States and European systems, agreement about the acceptability of the doctoral thesis has usually been arrived at in advance of the occasion. In the United Kingdom based systems, therefore, the viva may play a much more important part in determining the outcome for a doctoral candidate (although even here, it is not unknown for the examiners to have reached informally an agreed conclusion about the thesis in advance of the viva, although this view may change as a consequence of the event).

So what is the purpose of the viva? It fulfils a number of functions.

1. It reassures the examiners (and the university) that you actually did the work and wrote the thesis yourself.
2. It establishes your knowledge of the wider field so that you can place your work in this context.
3. It shows that you have become a wholly professional researcher who can make an original contribution to the development of knowledge in your field.
4. It removes any doubts and anxieties the examiners may have about the worthwhile nature of your work and about the research decisions that you made and which they may not fully understand from the text alone.

One problem in discussing the preparation that the candidate may undertake for the viva lies in the variability of the occasion. All institutions will have regulations relating to the conduct of the viva, and it is the candidate's responsibility to ensure that they are familiar with these. They may vary from faculty to faculty and even between departments and disciplines, but they will be available for scrutiny. The problem is that the regulations themselves will tell you nothing about what their meaning and application may involve in reality. Again, this may vary across faculties, departments and disciplines. Even within a given institution, and certainly across the university system as a whole, there is no one defined set of purposes and practices in relation to the role of the doctoral viva. The candidate is therefore confronted with inconsistencies and contradictions that it is not possible to resolve in a simple way. It is the case that no one can tell you in advance how long the viva will take – it may be three-quarters of an hour or six hours (although both these extremes – while not unknown – are exceptional). Two hours would be unexceptional. Nor can anyone tell you what the nature of the dialogue will be. In one case, a candidate may be told at the commencement of the viva that they will be awarded the degree, and the discussion may resolve itself into the best means of getting the research published. In another case, the candidate may be taken through every dot and comma of the thesis in a viva lasting several hours, to be presented at the end with a long list of required corrections – without the promise of the ultimate award of the degree.

Your thesis itself will have influenced the examiners' judgment – about what they need to focus on, and the way in which they need to do this. The personality of the respective examiners will be important, as will their relationship with each other (will one dominate?) and the relationship you build with them during the course of the viva.

In spite of these uncertainties, there are things you can do in advance of the viva to help your cause.

1. Make sure you familiarise yourself with the regulations of your institution relating to the conduct of the PhD viva. While there are large areas of commonality, regulations may vary between institutions and within institutions between different faculties, departments and disciplines. The regulations will include the notice of submission, which you may be required to give.
2. Make sure you are aware of the possible outcome of the viva. It may be any of the following.

(a) The immediate award of the degree may follow the viva without the need for any corrections or amendments. This is clearly the most desirable outcome and the one, which you will aim at, but it is not common.

(b) You may be required to make some minor corrections and amendments within a short period of time – perhaps one to three months – after which the degree will be awarded without a further viva. Usually, the corrections and amendments only have to be referred to the supervisor or internal examiner for approval rather then the external examiner. This is the most common outcome.

(c) You may be required to make major changes as a consequence of weaknesses that need to be addressed. This may involve a longer period of time – perhaps up to two years – although if your defence at the viva was sufficiently impressive and the changes made are appropriate, another viva may not necessarily be required. This is a disappointing outcome but the situation can be retrieved once you have overcome the emotional frustration and have gathered the material and psychological resources to address the problems, although it is advisable not to delay too long in doing this or the impetus may be lost for good.

(d) Occasionally, the thesis may be deemed adequate but the defence of it at the viva may be found wanting. The examiners may not have felt able to testify to the professional competence of the candidate in consequence. This may occur when perhaps the topic of the research is too narrow for the examiners to be able to confidently make this judgment. There may be the option for the examiners to set a written or practical examination in the field of study, subject, of course, to due notice, in order for them to be able to make the required judgment. You may be required to represent yourself for a second viva after perhaps six months or a year, during which time you can read more widely in the field of study and thus be in a better position to place the thesis in the appropriate context or to display a better understanding of its implications in the field of study.

(e) The thesis may be found not to be up to doctoral standard and the examiners may feel there is no way that it could be brought up to that standard, but they may feel it has reached the standard where they can award an MPhil degree. This is something of a consolation prize and means you do not go away entirely empty-handed, and there is still the possibility that you may be able to write one or two articles arising from it. However, it is still a disappointment that the thesis did not reach the required standard and there was no way that it could be amended to do so. You might be able to benefit from the experience and use it to make a better attempt next time, if you can muster the material and psychological resources, which is not always easy.

(f) The thesis may be totally rejected by the examiners without the possibility of resubmission. This absolute failure is relatively rare and should not occur given adequate supervision and it is often associated with external candidates who may not have had access to appropriate supervision. A supervisor should be in a position to counsel out of the system any student who seems to not have the intellectual or other capabilities required to successfully complete a PhD.

You should also be aware of the provisions for appeal in your institution. However, you must recognise that you are not able to appeal simply because you do not like the outcome. There must be some substance to your case. It may be that you can argue that the examiners appointed were not appropriate for the thesis e.g. political scientists were appointed to examine a thesis in public sector management and placed too much emphasis on their perspective, which was not entirely appropriate. Your case is weakened, of course, if you played a significant part in selecting the examiners. It must also be recognised that while further examiners may be appointed to re-evaluate the thesis a weak or marginal thesis is likely to remain just that and this is likely to be the conclusion of other examiners.

3. Ask your supervisor to clarify any point about which you may be uncertain. It may not always be possible for the supervisor to provide the clarification you seek – the information may not be available or known to the supervisor, or the supervisor may feel it is not appropriate or wise to respond at that stage or the questions may have more to do with issues of your confidence rather than lack of information. You should always feel free to ask elsewhere if you feel it is necessary.

4. Ask former PhD candidates from the department what their experience was, bearing in mind that it may have no relation to yours.

5. Ask another member of the department or faculty, a colleague, a fellow student, anyone who is likely to be able to do so usefully, to conduct a mock viva with you – preferably set up more than one – the more experience the better. Get them to debrief you at the end – what were your strengths and weaknesses, where did you hesitate or seem unsure of yourself. This can be invaluable in establishing the right air of confidence without being either too assertive or too defensive. Be prepared to reciprocate the favour.

6. Be prepared to suggest names of possible examiners if your institution invites you to do so. This may be done formally or informally. The practice varies between and even within institutions. This means doing your homework on the background of the various possibilities, bearing in mind that some may be unavailable or unwilling. You should of course discuss this with your supervisor, whose views will undoubtedly be sought in any event. It is helpful to know something about what they have written – you have probably referred to it in your thesis – their approach to research, their standing in the subject, the school of thought they belong to – are they likely to be sympathetic to your work? Do they have a particular reputation as an examiner? Are they known for aggressive questioning or do they prefer

a collegial discussion? You may not be able to establish the answers to all these questions but there is no harm in asking them. Can you find somebody with experience of them in the capacity of examiner? Do not be afraid to pursue the matter of the appointment of examiners. Ask your supervisor if the appropriate bodies within the institution have approved their appointment yet and if he or she does not know, ask the administrator concerned. Ask whether a date for the viva has yet been suggested or confirmed. You do not wish to be suddenly confronted with a near date that throws your plans for preparation into confusion. Nor do you wish the date to be postponed so far into the future as to increase the stress involved as well as the work of revision. Your request may even prompt some action.

7. Put into operation a systematic programme of preparation for the viva. This includes reading Partington et al. (1993) that will provide you with some insights into the questions examiners may ask on the various aspects of your thesis. For the purpose of undertaking systematic preparation for the viva, it would be useful to consult Phillips and Pugh (1994:140–142) where they present a useful schema for conducting both revision of the thesis and preparation for the viva at the same time. You should also consult Murray (2002:244–280) where she addresses many of the questions that candidates ask about their viva and how the event may be approached, questions anticipated and responses prepared.

Finally, while this may sound difficult if not impossible, try to regard the viva as a positive experience to be looked forward to. It is part of the learning process in the doctoral experience and may one day inform your own approach should you, in your turn, find yourself acting as a PhD examiner. The examiners will ask searching questions, will challenge you, perhaps criticise, and certainly debate with you. It is important to tell yourself that you know far more about this topic than they do and you should be in a position to confidently address their questions, while being careful not to appear too assertive or too defensive.

Remember that something like four out of five PhD theses are accepted at the viva, even though most will require some level of correction or amendment. Total failure is relatively rare. It is during the process of actually getting to the point where there is a thesis to submit that most PhD projects will fall by the wayside.

Tutorial

Progress questions

1. Why should you commence writing as a continuous activity as soon as possible?
2. What is likely to be the structure of chapters in your thesis?
3. What are the purposes of an Abstract, and what information is it likely to contain?
4. Why is the Introduction an important part of the thesis?
5. What does the Literature Review contribute to the thesis?
6. What is the distinction between 'research methods' and 'research methodology'?
7. What is the purpose of the Conclusion to your thesis?

Discussion points

1. Is it preferable to write in blocks of 500–1,000 words or do you favour more extended lengths of writing?
2. What kind of internal prompts are most likely to persuade you to begin and to continue writing?

Practical assignments

1. In relation to your current activities and commitments, try to establish a writing schedule that will enable you to write regularly and usefully.
2. Looking ahead, try to establish some writing milestones for at least the next year, and if possible, beyond.
3. Draft an Introduction to your thesis or to a thesis you are considering.

Study and revision tips

1. Read some Abstracts of theses or journal articles in your field of study and evaluate how well they describe the contents.

2. Read the Introductions to some theses in your field of study. Compare their contents and assess how well you feel each has opened the subsequent thesis.

3. Read and critique a number of Literature Reviews from theses in your field of study, making a note of common strengths and weaknesses.

4. Examine the Conclusions to various theses in your field of study and list for each what you consider makes each Conclusion weak or strong.

5. Look carefully at the manner in which different kinds of research data and findings have been presented in theses in your field of study.

9 **Presentation**

One-minute overview

It is essential to establish the requirements of your institution in terms of presentational detail, and to be aware of academic conventions, particularly in relation to your discipline. You need to evolve a clear and consistent style of writing with a limited use of headings and subheadings. The need for a formal mode of presentation with correct grammar, punctuation and spelling has to be emphasised, together with the appropriate presentation of tables and figures. It is also necessary to ensure that the required margins are left and that the binding conforms to the institution's regulations.

This final chapter will present some of the more important detail that you will need to successfully present a doctoral thesis. Some of the information may seem superfluous or trivial but many a thesis has been referred back for numerous corrections, a situation which could have been avoided or at least reduced in its burden by paying due attention to the necessary detail. There is also the possibility that for whatever reason those corrections may never be done. As always, you are reminded that it is absolutely essential to refer to the requirements of your particular institution in all these matters of detail in order to ensure that you comply with them or at least can provide a powerful reason for non-compliance where you consider this essential and the rules allow some leeway. You will also need to be aware of the conventions used in your particular discipline and to consult with your supervisor about any preferences he or she may have and the reasons for them. There are also

British Standard recommendations in existence for the presentation of higher degree theses and this may usefully be consulted.

Paper and pages

1. It is usual for A4 size paper to be used for theses (210mm x 297mm).
2. It is used in the vertical or portrait manner.
3. Only one side of the paper should be used.
4. It should be of sufficient quality to ensure that the print does not appear on the reverse side of the paper.
5. Where a table figure or diagram requires a page larger than A4 to be used, make sure the paper is folded in the vertical position, with the fold not more than 195mm from the left-hand edge of the paper and the folded section edge not less than 40mm from the left-hand edge of the paper. This will reduce the possibility of the fold being cut or the folded section edge being sewn in during binding.
6. Margins are needed to allow for binding, when sewing and trimming will occur.
7. The proportion of text to margin influences the visual appearance of the text for better or worse.
8. Margins must be used consistently throughout the thesis. The margins most commonly used are:

   (a) 20mm – top and right hand margins
   (b) 40mm – left-hand margins (this constitutes the spine)
   (c) 40mm – bottom margins.

There are some exceptions to this general rule. These exceptions are:

   (i) the Title Page;
   (ii) the Acknowledgements;
   (iii) chapter pages which are allocated 40mm as the top margin in order to allow for the title of the chapter;
   (iv) pages which contain tables, figures or diagrams of unusual proportions.

Pagination

1. It is a requirement for all doctoral theses that there is adequate pagination.
2. Pagination should be left until the thesis is finally completed and fully assembled. This avoids the need to constantly re-number and with modern word-processing does not present a considerable task at this stage.
3. In order to retain control over the assembling of the thesis, it is often helpful to mark page numbers in pencil as a temporary measure.
4. Remember to fill in any page numbers you have referred to in the text but were unable to complete at that time.
5. Consecutive numbering of pages throughout the entire thesis is normally required.
6. Use Arabic numerals.
7. The Title page is designated as page 1 but is not itself commonly numbered.
8. Place the page numbers below the text 20mm from the bottom of the page and centred between the lines of the margins, 110mm from the left-hand edge of the paper.
9. As the thesis is numbered consecutively throughout, if you should include any appendices which carry page numbers from their previous publication then these would need to be re-numbered in accordance with the sequence of which they are now a part.

Writing style

1. An appropriate style of writing needs to be used consistently throughout the thesis.
2. Clear and effective communication of the research and its findings is essential if the thesis is to have any value.
3. This communication must be undertaken in a way which is clear and objective, and which provides a dispassionate account.
4. Narrative or text will be the medium through which you will communicate the bulk of what you wish to say.
5. The text needs to be clear and logical even when it is technically or conceptually complex.

6. The clear presentation of important findings on the basis of cogent analysis of evidence will ensure a thesis that is neither dull nor pedantic- its interest will grasp the reader.

7. Use short clear sentences for coherence – say 20–25 words in length as far as possible. Do not write in a way that involves circumlocution or in a complicated style on the mistaken assumption that this is the 'academic' approach.

8. Bear in mind that it should be notionally possible for the reader to be able to replicate your research from the reading of it, even though in many cases, particularly in some areas of the social sciences, practical difficulties will make this impossible. For this purpose, a clear and unambiguous account is necessary.

9. The presence of ambiguity may suggest that there is confusion and imprecision in the mind of the candidate.

The thesis is essentially a grouping of ideas and data into a coherent sequence.

1. Develop your own way of organizing material into this logical sequence.

2. Begin by drawing up a draft outline of the entire thesis.

3. Such a draft of how you intend to develop the presentation of the thesis may provide you with some indication of

   (a) possible omissions;
   (b) where the order of the thesis material needs to be changed;
   (c) where some changes of emphasis need to be made.

These adjustments can be made while the thesis is still at a stage where frequent revision and adjustment is an important part of the process.

4. Do not expect to sit down and write the thesis from beginning to end.

   (a) Different parts will be written at different times.
   (b) Revision of the different parts will also go on at different times.

(c) Such revision of particular parts may have impacts upon other parts where further revisions may need to be made.

(d) Such revisions may involve changing the sequence in which the material is presented.

(e) As suggested above, the Introduction may be the first thing to be written – and also the last, as you can see the thesis as a whole and can give the reader a clear road map in the Introduction.

Make sure you consider the following points in your writing. This will aid your reader and in particular your examiners to read the thesis and understand exactly what you mean.

1. Provide a clear heading to each section indicating its content. However, try to avoid using more than three levels of heading at most, as more will tend to fragment the text.
2. Ensure these headings are presented in a uniform manner in relation to

   (a) grammar and sentence construction
   (b) use of capital letters.

3. Identify formulae in a numerical sequence within the section in which they are used for ease of reference.
4. Define any technical or unfamiliar terms in the text when they are first used or alternatively make their meaning apparent by the way you use them.
5. Use terminology consistently so that you do not employ a particular term in one way and then use it with a different meaning elsewhere in the text.
6. Report the thesis in the past tense – it is an account of what happened.
7. Use the present tense only when referring the reader to such evidence as tables or figures presented in the text.
8. Present the thesis in a formal manner – do not use the vernacular or colloquial expressions unless quoting directly. Remember that written language differs from spoken language. If you feel obliged for any reason to use a piece of colloquial English, then place it in inverted commas to indicate its status.

9. Write in the impersonal. Use the third person. Avoid the personal pronouns (I, me, you, we, us) except in some kinds of qualitative research e.g. when a diary may have been kept as part of the data collection techniques. Do not use such expressions as 'One observes that...' or 'The author considered that...'

10. Avoid spelling mistakes – there is no excuse for them. Do not hesitate to make frequent use of a good dictionary if you are in any doubt at all. Spell checkers are helpful but do not necessarily provide the complete answer. There is no substitute for asking a competent third party to read a draft and point out any possible errors or queries. Note that many spell checkers on word processors use American English. The use of American English is at best variably accepted in the UK and is preferably avoided. Make sure you use an English spell checker.

11. Do not use simplified spellings such as 'altho' or 'tele' – a thesis is a formal document.

12. Avoid errors in grammar and punctuation – again a competent reader for your draft can help here. Keep a suitable book on grammar and punctuation beside you.

13. Repetition of words and phrases is tedious for the reader and represents poor writing style. An appropriate thesaurus and a book of synonyms and antonyms will be invaluable.

14. Where acronyms or abbreviations are used, the name or title must be presented in full on its initial occurrence, with the abbreviation placed in brackets behind it e.g. Doctor of Philosophy (PhD). Subsequently, the abbreviation alone can be used.

15. Otherwise, abbreviations are not used in the text of a thesis. Some common abbreviations may be used in

   – bibliographic references
   – footnotes
   – endnotes
   – tables
   – appendices
   – the bibliography.

16. Note that symbols may be used in tables e.g.' %' but would need to be presented in literal form in the text e.g.' per cent'.

Let us now examine some of the above points in more detail.

Headings and subheadings

The organisation of a thesis is essentially focused around chapters. A chapter contains a central theme around which concepts, ideas, data and information are organised in a coherent way to convey important issues to the reader. As the amount of material and its complexity varies from chapter to chapter, so does the length of the various chapters. Many good doctoral theses are organised solely on the basis of chapters without any further subdivision below this level.

Increasingly, however, there has emerged a tendency in recent years to subdivide chapters into headings and subheadings, perhaps reflecting a tendency for doctoral theses to increase in length and complexity. Subdivision below the chapter level has two benefits.

1. It enables the reader to hold short compact sections more easily in the memory.
2. It provides cues or signals as to the argument that is being presented, making it easier to follow.

However, as Dunleavy (2003) has pointed out, three common errors occur in dividing up chapters.

1. Chapters may be under-organised i.e. be provided with headings which do not function in a useful way because they

    (a) involve some sections which are much longer or much shorter than others;
    (b) use the same order of heading for each of these sections, particularly the often relatively short Introduction and Conclusion for each chapter.

The resulting lack of balance can confuse readers.

2. Chapters may be over-organised with

   (a) too many levels of heading and subheading (with third or fourth order headings);
   (b) insufficient distinction in font size and appearance;
   (c) complicated numbering systems.

A system that numbers paragraphs in a report very usefully may create frustration and confusion in a long doctoral text. If you decide to use a numbering system at all (and you may prefer to rely on emphasis, font size and the location of different orders of heading to provide structure within a chapter) then it is a good rule of thumb not to go beyond numbering the main sections in chapters e.g. 2.1 or 2.2 and never go to 2.1.2, 2.1.3 or beyond. For example, a chapter 4 in your thesis concerned with research methods might look like this.

4.1 Introduction that outlines the contents of the chapter and the main lines of the discussion that will be explored.

4.2 Justification – why the particular approach was adopted, the chosen type of method and the investigative technique.

4.3 Research procedures – how the investigation was planned and implemented.

4.4 Ethical issues.

4.5 Summary of the chapter including a signpost to the analysis and results, which will be the subject of the next chapter.

3. Chapters may be provided with different systems of headings at different points in the thesis. This may commonly arise because different chapters are written at different points in the process and ideas about appropriate headings and their usage may change as the thesis progresses but any revision of the earlier usages may be overlooked. The scheme of headings needs to remain the same throughout the thesis, with flexibility provided where required by the use of third-order headings beyond the

initial first- and second-order headings to enable you to cope with longer chapters with more extended sections or more complicated data or argument. Consistency is the key to the provision of useful headings in a thesis.

In providing headings, you need to ensure the following principles are applied.

1. Ensure each heading contributes to indicating your line of argument to the reader. A heading should indicate what you are going to argue about the topic in question i.e. where the discussion is going to get to. Vague, formalistic, process orientated headings lacking in specific substance merely serve to mislead or confuse the reader.
2. Do not use questions as headings. The questions involved and which are being answered may very usefully have been identified earlier in the research process, but the thesis itself needs to be focused on providing substantive answers to these questions.
3. Avoid inaccurate headings – a section must not claim to do something it does not do – and it is often difficult for an author to see that the text does not do something they had intended it to. Do not make implied claims in your headings that the text does not or cannot live up to. The heading should be commensurate with the contents of the text.
4. Headings, which repeat words or phrases – particularly those taken from your thesis title and/or its theoretical/thematic concepts – should be avoided. Such headings serve only to both bore and confuse the reader – it does nothing to link together the various parts of the thesis.

Note that chapter headings

1. indicate succinctly the area of the thesis the chapter focuses on;
2. are numbered consecutively in Arabic numerals;
3. allow two line spaces between chapter number and heading;
4. use single line spacing if longer than one line;
5. are capitalised for the chapter number and heading as in the example below.

CHAPTER 4

RESEARCH METHODS: A QUALITATIVE APPROACH TO THE PROBLEM

It should be noted that chapter subheadings are:

1. numbered throughout the chapter in consistent format;
2. not capitalised as in the example below.

4.3 Research procedures

Both chapter headings and subheadings appear in the List of Contents at the beginning of the thesis in the exact form in which they appear in the text.

Grammar, spelling and punctuation

Most of us have weaknesses in our knowledge and application of the rules of grammar, spelling and punctuation. It is quite likely that we are unaware of some of them. However, it must be recognised that inadequate attention to these matters may seriously undermine the impact of our thesis and the quality of the research it contains. A negative impression conveyed by the lack of attention to the importance of grammar, spelling and punctuation may result in an outcome where extensive corrections are required by the examiners, particularly if as a consequence of poor presentation, the precise meaning of some important element in the thesis is rendered ambiguous or unclear. In presenting any mathematical or statistical content in the thesis you would take great pains to ensure their correct use. Equally in writing, even if it is scientifically or technologically based, grammar, spelling and punctuation must be used correctly to provide the necessary clarity and precision.

Grammar

This is probably not the time at which to contemplate undertaking a revision course in English grammar, even if you could succeed in overcoming the potential embarrassment entailed in acknowledging its desirability. You may therefore settle for keeping a good reference book on the subject by your desk. There are, however, a number of elementary things which you can check as you write your thesis as well as in the process of revision. Utilising a running check on the grammar as a form of quality control certainly reduces the burden of the revision process. You should bear in mind that the majority of errors arise from a failure to identify fairly simple mistakes.

Use the following rules as a checklist to run over your writing at regular intervals so that the amount you have to do on each occasion does not become wearisome.

1. Your sentences must be complete.
2. Use the simplest practical grammatical construction.
3. Keep your sentences short rather than long – ideally 20–25 words and no more then 40.
4. If your draft sentence runs to more then 40 words, break it down into two or three sentences.
5. Sentences should contain a subject, verb and usually an object.
6. The subject, verb and object must be clearly identified.
7. The subject of the verb must be clearly identified and the use of

    (a) the passive form e.g. 'It was argued that' and
    (b) the use of implied subjects as in 'This involved..' where there is no subject noun identified should be avoided.

8. The main verb must be clearly identified and shown to be such by highlighting it by its place in the sentence structure to ensure it is clearly more important than any secondary verbs used.
9. Nothing should be interposed between subject, verb and object.
10. This core of subject, verb and object should be placed in the middle of the sentence after any introductory or qualifying clauses.

11. Any qualifying or subordinate clauses should be placed at the beginning or end of the sentence.

12. Other words or phrases used in the sentence e.g. adjectives or adjectival clauses should usually be placed before or after the core subject – verb – object.

13. Use the correct tense for the verb. In writing your thesis you write in the past tense as you are referring to what has been done. The present tense is used only in referring the reader to tables, figures or similar evidence placed in the text.

14. Ensure that each sentence adds something of substance to your thesis except for a necessary few that will provide linkage and continuity at appropriate points in the thesis.

Following the above rules will help you to avoid the damaging possibility of presenting your argument in a misleading form or advancing propositions in a way you did not intend. This would undermine your thesis and reduce your chances of success significantly.

Spelling

1. Poor spelling in a thesis is unacceptable and unnecessary.

2. The need for ready access to a good dictionary has already been pointed out.

3. The need to use a spell-checker that does not employ American English or other forms of English inappropriately has already been mentioned.

4. Bear in mind that a spell-checker does not recognise as incorrect a valid spelling of a word which is inappropriate in relation to its meaning in the sentence within which it is placed. Common examples are 'there' instead of 'their, or 'were' instead of 'where'.

5. The use of a spell-checker does not eliminate the need for a careful reading at draft stage, preferably with the help of an independent reader.

6. Avoid simplified spellings such as 'thro', 'phone', 'tho', 'altho', 'tele', 'mobile' (for mobile telephone). Simplified spellings are unacceptable in a thesis.

7. Use of a thesaurus or book of synonyms will ensure that you do not have to repeat the same words or phrases too often.

8. It is the case that a small number of words tend to be responsible for the vast majority of spelling mistakes in thesis writing.

9. Another common error in theses is that some words tend to be mis-used because their meaning has not been properly understood.

Punctuation

Correct punctuation is essential to ensure that the writing in the text is clear as to its meaning. While punctuation has tended to become simpler in recent years, it still performs a significant function, and the most important accepted practices are listed below.

The full stop is used

(a) to end sentences
(b) after most abbreviations (except in the case of some international bodies such as UNESCO, NATO or the EU).

Note that in modern usage the initial letters of the names of groups or organisations with no full stop (period) between the letters is considered acceptable e.g. BA, BBC, MA, MP, RAF, PhD.

A comma or some other form of punctuation may follow a full stop if the abbreviation occurs within a sentence e.g. *Two years after gaining his Ph.D., he obtained a research post.*

If the abbreviation occurs at the end of a sentence, only the full stop is necessary e.g. *The battle of Marathon was fought in 490 B.C.*

If the sentence is in the form of a question or an exclamation, the full stop for the abbreviation will be followed by a question mark or an exclamation mark e.g.*Was the battle of Marathon fought in 490 B.C.? What a waste of a good Ph.D.!*

Commas are used in the following circumstances.

(a) To separate independent clauses linked by a conjunction e.g. '*the research process was lengthy, but eventually she earned her Ph.D.*'

(b) To separate items in a series e.g. *'John succeeded in his research, in his viva, and in obtaining a research post at the university.'*

(c) To separate parallel modifiers e.g. *'he set out on the long, lonely research programme to his Ph.D.'*

(d) To set off non-restrictive elements e.g. *'Statistics, which are more a symbol of information than understanding, seldom appeared in his research work.'* (An example of a restrictive element would be *'Statistics which mislead are dangerous.'*)

(e) To indicate an introductory phrase e.g. *'With his entire research programme undermined, John abandoned his Ph.D.'*

(f) To indicate a subordinate clause e.g. *'If John had listened to his supervisor, he might have produced research of a higher quality.'*

(g) To set off interrupting elements e.g. *'Mary, on the other hand, preferred to use qualitative research methods.'*

(h) To provide clarity e.g. *'After analysis, the data were stored on disk.'*

Semicolons

Use these in the following circumstances.

(a) Where independent clauses are not linked by a conjunction (e.g. and, but, or, nor, for, so, yet) e.g. ' *Mary was greatly impressed by her supervisor; she copied his methods meticulously.'*

(b) Where independent clauses are connected by a conjunctive adverb (e.g. however, nevertheless, then, moreover, consequently) e.g. *'John assiduously recorded events as they occurred in his field research; however, an accurate record is not the only concern.'*

(c) Where independent clauses are connected by a phrase which modifies the sentence (e.g. in fact, for example, on the other hand, in the first place) e.g. *'The research programme was a recent innovation; in fact, its impetus derived from the appointment of a new professor.'*

(d) Where items need to be separated in a sentence in which commas are also extensively used e.g. *'The research seminar consisted of three presenters: a research student at the university, understood to have strong views on the subject; a visiting guest speaker, thought to have an opposing view; and a professor at the university, considered to be something of an authority on the subject.'*

Colons

Note that it is good practice to leave one space after a colon, unless it is used to express time e.g. 11:35 a.m.

(a) Use a colon after a clause has formally introduced a passage e.g. *'The research design consisted of a wide variety of methods: quantitative and qualitative, including interviews, questionnaires, and participant observation.'*

(b) A colon may indicate that what follows is an example e.g. *'Different kinds of research methods were separately reviewed by individual students: quantitative by John, qualitative by Mary, and ethnographic by William.'*

(c) A colon may indicate that what follows is an explanation of what has just been presented e.g. a book title on research methods reads *Survey Research: a Decisional Approach.*

(d) A colon may indicate that what follows is an elaboration of what has gone before e.g. *'Grounded theory is more than a phenomenological method: it is a systematic set of procedures with which to develop an inductively derived grounded theory about a phenomenon.'*

Dash

The dash is used with no space preceding or following.

(a) It surrounds material which is essentially parenthetical and which interrupts the flow of the text e.g. Research is inquiry-systematic, critical and empirical-into some aspect of the physical, natural and social world.

(b) It may be used as a form of summarizing e.g. Weber, Parsons, Durkheim, Merton-all were distinguished sociologists.

(c) It may be used to provide emphasis e.g. The development of Sociology stems from one man-Comte.

Parentheses

These are used for the following purposes.

(a) To enclose material that explains a preceding point e.g. Case study research (an over-used method) describes and investigates the variables and relationships involved in a particular group or institution.

(b) To enclose material that amplifies something that has gone before e.g. Basil Cameron (1884–1975) was a once-famous British orchestral conductor.

(c) To enclose a series or list containing a number of items e.g. Several results are possible as a consequence of a PhD examination (1) pass, (2) fail, (3) deferred, (4) referred for corrections.

Note: A parenthesis contained within another sentence does not

(a) start with a capital letter;
(b) end with a full stop.

A sentence that is essentially a parenthesis between other sentences has both e.g. John went on to the internet. (He did this often.) He went to his favourite search engine.

Square Brackets may be used in the following circumstances.

(a) To enclose a parenthesis within a statement that is already parenthetical e.g. It is in work like that of Marsh (The Changing Social Structure of England and Wales [Routledge and Kegan Paul, 1965]) that a clear analysis of the changing pattern of crime can be obtained.

(b) To enclose an interpolation in a quotation e.g. the critical review was entitled "A Cassual [sic] Analysis of Statistical Errors in PhD Theses."

Slash

This is used to separate

(a) lines of poetry
(b) dates e.g. 01/05/48 (1 May 1948)
(c) alternative words e.g. the thesis must be failed and/or re-written.

Quotation marks

These perform the following functions.

(a) They enclose the exact words written or spoken by someone else.
(b) They indicate dialogue.
(c) They draw attention to some particular word.
(d) They enclose in parenthesis English translations of words, phrases or sentences in another language.
(e) They enclose any words or phrases that are used in some special sense as in 'The term "bureaucracy" is usually applied to central government and municipal administration, as is also the term "red tape".'

Question marks

These are used

(a) after a direct question;
(b) to indicate a doubtful figure or date e.g. Anne Boleyn (1507?–1536) was the second wife of Henry VIII.

Exclamation marks

These are used to express

(a) a command e.g. open the test paper. Begin!
(b) surprise e.g. abandon my research? Never!
(c) Disbelief e.g. these data have been fabricated!
(d) Anger e.g. stop plagiarizing my research questions!

Note:

(i) Do not follow an exclamation mark with a comma or full stop.

(ii) Do not make too much use of exclamation marks e.g. to display relatively mild expressions of feelings.

Apostrophe

This is used for the following purposes.

(a) To form the possessive case of nouns not ending in s. These may be singular or plural nouns.

Singular	**Plural**
The supervisor's role is to give advice.	The children's test results provided useful data.

(b) To form the possessive case of singular nouns ending in s either (i) by adding's or (ii) by using an apostrophe.

The rule of thumb here is to add's to monosyllabic names such as Phipps or Marx where the sibilant ending makes this desirable (thus Phipps's or Marx's).

For multisyllabic names, only an apostrophe is added to the name (thus Dickens' or Socrates').

Where names end in a silent s, the possessive is formed by adding an's e.g. Camus's .

(c) To form the possessive of plural nouns ending in s e.g. the data was drawn from the psychological tests' results.

(d) To indicate joint possession by adding's to the last name only e.g. critics acclaimed Arthur Sullivan and W.S. Gilbert's comic operas.

(e) To indicate an omission e.g. the swinging '60s or the research interview started at nine o'clock.

(f) To form the plural of numerals, letters and words e.g. because of his poor writing all his 7's looked like t's. In his paper he used too many however's.

Never use an apostrophe with

  (i) the possessive case of the personal pronoun i.e. its not it's and theirs not their's
 (ii) ordinary plurals e.g. five research workers were employed
(iii) inanimate objects e.g. say 'the closure of the research unit' not the research unit's closure.

You can always replace the use of the apostrophe by 'of the' e.g. 'the researcher's work' by 'the work of the researcher'.

Hyphen

The practice in the use of the hyphen is often inconsistent, and if in any doubt, you should consult a good dictionary or grammar book.

These are the common usages.

(a) To form a compound adjective preceding a noun e.g. a well-earned doctorate.
    The hyphen is not used when the first word is an adverb ending in – ly e.g. a correctly written thesis.
    No hyphen is required when the compound adjective is preceded by the noun e.g. the thesis is well written.
(b) To connect prefixes to capitalised words e.g. pre-Edwardian or post-Thatcher.
(c) To link compound nouns e.g. Brahms was a conductor-composer.

Numerals

(a) If the number cannot be spelled out using two words or less, use the numeral.
(b) Dates and page numbers are not normally spelt out e.g. 'December 25' or '25 December' and 'page 47' rather than 'the twenty-fifth of December' and 'the forty-seventh page'.

(c) Numerals never begin a sentence e.g. '*31,000 people completed the questionnaire*' should become '*The questionnaire was completed by 31,000 people*'.

Percentage and money

(a) Figures or amounts are spelled out if they can be written in two words or less.
(b) If more than two words are required, then figures or amounts should be given as numerals, e.g.

spell out fifteenth percentile; seventy-two percent; ten Euros; forty pounds Sterling; twenty-one US dollars.

Use numerals for 141%; 72.5%; 114 Euros; £500 Sterling; $121.

Dates

(a) Be consistent in how you write dates either '14 October 1938' or 'October 14, 1938' but do not mix the use of both of these in the thesis.
(b) Either 'May 1938' or 'May, 1938,' is acceptable, but not both in the same thesis.
(c) If a comma is used between month and year, a comma must follow the year also unless some other form of punctuation is required e.g. a full stop.
(d) Express centuries in lower case e.g. in the fifteenth century.
(e) A hyphen is used to express the century as an adjective e.g. sixteenth century agriculture.
(f) Write decades as either 'in the forties' or in numerals e.g. ' in the 1940s'.
(g) The term 'B.C.' (Before Christ) follows the year whereas 'A.D.' (after the birth of Christ) precedes the year e.g. 'In 44 B.C. Claudius invaded Britain' and 'In A.D. 1485 Richard III lost the battle of Bosworth'.
(h) In using a Western and a non-Western date, use a parenthesis for one or the other e.g. 1798 (Year Four of the Republic).

(i) Both 'in 1889–90' and 'from 1889 to 1890' are acceptable as is '1889–90 to 1929–30'.

(j) Do not write 'from 1974–1997' as the absence of the preposition 'to' may create confusion. Write '1974 to 1997'.

Consecutive numbers

(a) In connecting two numbers write the second number in full for all numbers from one up to ninety-nine e.g. 5–6; 13–16; 24–87.

(b) From one hundred onwards give only the last two digits of the second number if it is within the same hundred or thousand e.g. 106–07; 121–32; 1, 320–64; 15,721–78.

(c) Otherwise write 461–537; 881–1017; 1,521–624; 1,759–1,827; 16,721–17,014.

(d) For the sake of clarity, where for a number in the thousands a single digit would be dropped, it may be retained e.g. 1,718–1,827.

Roman numerals

Capital Roman numerals are used for the following.

(a) Main headings e.g. in the outline of a thesis.

(b) For works which are divided into volumes e.g. Volume II of *Encyclopaedia Britannica*.

(c) For Books and Parts of major works e.g. Book I of Plato's *Republic* or Part II of Plater's *Beiderbecke Trilogy*.

(d) For Acts of a play e.g. Act III of *Macbeth*.

(e) For people in a series such as monarchs where a common name is shared e.g. William III.

Lower case Roman numerals are used in the following instances.

(a) Chapters in a book e.g. Chapter vii of *Pride and Prejudice*.

(b) Scenes of a play e.g. Act II, Scene ii of *Macbeth*.

(c) Cantos of a poem e.g. Book II Canto iii of *The Faerie Queene*.

(d) Chapters of books in the Bible e.g. Luke xi.

(e) Pages from prefaces, forwards or introductions to books e.g. Page viii from Preface to *Churchill: the Member for Woodford*.

Tables

These are

(a) labelled clearly and exactly with the contents of the table;
(b) numbered using Arabic numerals;
(c) captioned.

Above the table

(a) allow two spaces between the table number and heading;
(b) type both the table number and the heading in capital letters;
(c) if the heading is longer than one line then it is single spaced;
(d) use the table number to refer to it in the text i.e. 'as shown in Table 2' rather than 'as shown in the following table'.

Beneath the table are placed

(a) the source
(b) any accompanying notes.

Notes to tables are indicated with asterisks, crosses and lower-case letters so that any possible confusion with textual notes including endnotes and footnotes is avoided.

If a table is taken from another source it is referred to in the thesis as a figure and is not numbered as part of the table sequence and the source is indicated beneath the table e.g.

Source: Nash (1981), p.179.

In the List of Tables the headings are included exactly as they appear above the tables in the text.

Tables

(a) present statistical data clearly and succinctly;
(b) assist the reader in detecting (i) relationships (ii) the significance of data (iii) the importance of proportions;
(c) avoid the need for lengthy prose explanations and interpretations.

A table is positioned in the text

(a) after the first reference to it in the text;
(b) normally at the end of the relevant paragraph;
(c) or if (b) is not possible at the end of the first paragraph on the following page;
(d) so that it is kept within normal page margins;
(e) so that if it is longer than one half of the vertical margins it is centred on a page of its own;
(f) so that if it is longer than a page it is centred on the next and, if necessary, subsequent pages, with the column headings repeated exactly on each page;
(g) so that if it is too wide to be presented vertically, it may be read from the spine down by placing it horizontally, ensuring that the margin at the top of the table remains at 40mm for a left hand margin.

All description of data within a table must be

(i) complete (ii) accurate (iii) brief (iv) consistent in style throughout the text (v) presented in the same grammatical structure in any given table.

Note.

(a) Abbreviations are kept to a minimum.
(b) Long column headings may be typed 'broadside' so they can be read from the bottom to the top of the page.

Lines and rules

(a) are only used if they help to group data in some specific way or ways;
(b) are used to separate row and column headings from the statistics;

Table 11 Changes in public transport traffic, staff and wages, Great Britain 1967–1977

(%)	Public road passenger transport	British BR
Traffic units*	−8.6	−5.1
Staff numbers	−13.1	−15.2
Traffic units per man	+5.2	+11.9
Real average earnings	+39.2	+36.1
Staff cost per traffic unit	+32.3	+21.6

* Passenger miles plus freight ton-miles.
† National Bus Company only (Source: Annual Reports)
Source: Department of Transport (1979).
Comparable data is not available for road freight transport.

(c) are used to separate totals from the statistics.

Side rules are not normally required.

An example of a typical table is shown.

Figures

These include

- bar graphs
- charts
- diagrams
- histograms
- illustrations
- line graphs
- maps
- photographs
- tables taken from another source or publications.

It is important to observe the following points in relation to figures.

1. Figures should be numbered sequentially with Arabic numerals.

2. Each figure should be captioned using capital letters as for a title e.g. Figure 15 Production Possibilities in the United Kingdom.

3. The source of the figure and any notes are normally placed below the figure.

4. A reader is entitled to assume the figure or illustration is your own work if no source is indicated.

5. Notes to figures and illustrations may be indicated with asterisks, crosses or lower-case letters so that possible confusion with endnote or footnote numbers in the text is avoided.

6. Figures normally follow the first reference to them in the text at the end of the relevant paragraph.

7. If this is not possible e.g. for reasons of space limitation, the figure or illustration is normally placed on the following page at the end of the first paragraph.

8. If a figure or illustration would occupy more than half of the printed area on that page, it should be placed on the next page.

9. Figures or illustrations should not go beyond the normal page margins.

10. Figures and illustrations are centred within the margins.

11. Most figures can now be reduced to fit within the normal margins by means of modern technology, but may be followed within the normal vertical dimensions with the fold not more than the 195mm from the left-hand edge of the paper and the folded section edge not less than 40mm from the left-hand edge of the paper. This enables the cutting and sewing processes involved in binding to take place without damaging the figure or illustration.

12. If two figures or illustrations are included on the same page, whether this is done vertically or horizontally, they should appear symmetrically.

13. The heading should state exactly what the figure or illustration shows.

14. Single space headings longer than one line.

15. Allow two line spaces between the number of the figure or illustration and the heading.

16. The heading may be placed below the illustration, diagram or photograph, following directly on the same line as the number of the figure.

17. Figures or illustrations are referred to in the text by their numbers e.g. 'as Figure 12 demonstrates.'

Binding

Your thesis will need to be bound, probably for the purposes of submission, although some universities do not require this until after the thesis has been accepted in order to facilitate corrections.

You must be careful to acquaint yourself with the requirements of your university in relation to the binding of the thesis e.g. how and where your name and initials together with the qualification and year of submission should appear – whether on the spine and/or front board. Detailed regulations may exist on whether the thesis is bound in cloth or linen, and what colour the covering should be. There may also be regulations covering the typeface, layout and the tooling of the lettering. Often, the university will have a recommended bookbinder or list of bookbinders, who will be aware of all the regulations and can be consulted regarding any unusual requirements.

Your thesis is now ready for submission. Good luck!

Tutorial

Progress questions

1. What are the main elements involved in establishing an appropriate writing style?
2. How would you develop the grouping of ideas and data into a coherent sequence in your thesis?
3. What considerations are important in developing a system of headings and subheadings?

Discussion point

1. To what extent do you think that the emphasis on correct grammar, punctuation and spelling is justified in a doctoral thesis?

Practical assignments

1. Check out your institution's requirements for doctoral theses relating to the Title Page, margins and binding. Look at some previously presented doctoral theses in your field, and in your institution, to see how these matters were handled.
2. Buy yourself, or ensure you have ready access to, a good dictionary, a book on English grammar, a thesaurus, and a book of synonyms and antonyms.
3. Make sure you have a UK English spell checker for submissions to a UK university.

Study tips and revision

1. Practice presenting tables and figures appropriately in context.
2. Familiarise yourself with abbreviations that are commonly used in doctoral theses, particularly in bibliographies.

Conclusion

So now you have your PhD. For some of you this will be the end of the road. You will go on to careers in industry, commerce, administration or the practice of a profession and never again undertake a task of this kind. You may find no reason to seek to publish your work beyond the shelves of the library or to pursue the interesting suggestions for further research or intriguing byways that your work produced. By the time you actually receive your degree your life may have moved in other directions, or if you pursued your research part-time, your full-time career may once again have taken over. If your doctorate is the pathway to an academic career, then you will now wish to optimise the publication possibilities from your thesis and to seek the resources to pursue those further research possibilities. What you need to do to achieve publication is beyond the scope of this book, but Berry (1994), Davis and Parker (1997), Coombes (2001), Kane and O'Reilly-De Brun (2001), Wolcott (2001), Murray (2002), Dunleavy (2003) and Marshall and Green (2004) all have useful suggestions to make.

You will, of course, have realised that your research is incomplete. More questions will have been raised than there are answers. Time will not permit even the most interesting issues to be pursued to the extent you might have wished. Even if you reject the notion of continuing with your research and feel that you are weary with both the subject and the process and never intend to return to either again, you will be able to reflect on what you have learnt and apply some of this usefully in your career, and on how pursuing even the narrowest of topics enabled you to widen both your experience and your horizons. There may be a lack of tangible rewards in terms of money, promotion or even secure employment, but the skills, contacts and expertise you have acquired may prove invaluable. There is also the qualification itself – a supreme academic achievement and a badge of title you can wear with pride throughout the rest of your life. There is also the knowledge that however large or small – whether you discovered pulsars or merely attempted to tweak a formula in an attempt to improve survey data in an input-output study in economics – you have made a contribution and one that has been recognised and acknowledged by those who are now your peers.

Further reading

Allison, B. (1997). *The Student's Guide to Preparing Dissertations and Theses*. London: Kogan Page.

Bell, J. (1993). *Doing Your Research Project*. Buckingham: Open University Press.

Berry, R. (1994). *The Research Project: How to Write It*. London: Routledge.

Brause, R. (2000). *Writing Your Doctoral Dissertation*. London: Falmer Press.

British Standards Institute (1990). *Recommendations for the Presentation of Theses and Dissertations*. BS 4821. London: British Standards Institute.

Burnard, P. and Morrison, P. (1990). *Nursing Research in Action*. Basingstoke: Macmillan.

Coombes, H. (2001). *Research Using IT*. Basingstoke: Palgrave.

Davis, G.B. and Parker, C.A. (1997). *Writing the Doctoral Dissertation*. New York: Barron's Educational Series, Inc.

Diamantopoulos, A. and Ashlegelmilch, B.B. (2000). *Taking the Fear Out of Data Analysis*. London: Thomson Learning.

Dunleavy, P. (2003). *Authoring a PhD*. Basingstoke: Palgrave Macmillan.

Gill, J. and Johnson, P. (1997). *Research Methods for Managers*. London: Paul Chapman Publishing.

Howard, K. and Sharp, J.A. (1983). *The Management of a Student Research Project*. Aldershot: Gower.

Hussey, J. and Hussey, R. (1997). *Business Research*. Basingstoke: Macmillan.

Kane, E. (1984). *Doing Your Own Research*. London: Marion Boyars.

Kane, E. and O'Reilly-De Brun, M. (2001). *Doing Your Own Research*. London: Marion Boyars.

Marshall, S. and Green, N. (2004) *Your PhD Companion.* Oxford: How To Books.

Murray, R. (2002). *How to Write a Thesis.* Maidenhead: Open University Press.

Phillips, E.M. and Pugh, D.S. (1994) *How to Get a PhD.* Buckingham: Open University Press.

Reid, N.G. and Bore, J.R.P. (1987) *Research Methods and Statistics in Health Care.* London: Edward Arnold.

Rudestam, K.E. and Newton, R.R. (2001) *Surviving Your Dissertation.* London: Sage.

Swetnam, D. (1997) *Writing Your Dissertation.* Oxford: How To Books Ltd.

Winkler, A.C. and McCuen, J.R. (1979). *Writing the research paper: A handbook.* New York: Harcourt Brace Jovanovich.

Wolcott, H.F. (2001) *Writing Up Qualitative Research.* London: Sage.

References

Argyris, C., Putman, R. and Smith, D.M. (1985). *Action Science.* San Francisco: Jossey-Bass.

Bouma, G.D. and Atkinson, G.B.J. (1995). *A Handbook of Social Science Research.* Oxford: Oxford University Press.

Cresswell, J.W. (1994). *Research Design: Quantitative and Qualitative Approaches.* London: Sage.

Feldman, R.S. (1990). *The Social Psychology of Education.* Cambridge: Cambridge University Press.

Gilbaldi, J. (1999). *MLA Handbook for Writers of Research Papers.* New York: Modern Language Association of America.

Giorgi, A. (1985). *Phenomenology and Psychological Research.* New York: Harper and Row.

Glaser, B.G. and Strauss, A.L. (1967). *The Discovery of Grounded Theory: Strategies for Qualitative Research.* Chicago: Aldine/Atherton.

Glass, G.V. (1976). Primary, Secondary, and Meta-analysis of Research. *Educational Researcher,* 5(10), 3–8.

Goffman, E. (1961). *Asylums.* New York: Doubleday.

Greenwood, D. and Lewin, M. (1998). *Introduction to Action Research: Social Research for Social Change.* Thousand Oaks: Sage.

Hamel J., Dufour, S. and Fortin, D. (1994). *Case Study Methods.* Thousand Oaks: Sage.

Harnack, A. and Kleppinger, E. (1997). Online: *The Internet Guide for Students and Writers.* New York: St. Martins.

Howard K. (ed.) (1978). *Managing a Thesis.* Bradford: University of Bradford Management Centre.

Human and Organisation Development Program of the Fielding Institute (HOD). (1998). *Inquiry and Research Knowledge Study Guide of the Human and Organisation Development Program of the Fielding Institute.* Santa Barbara: The Fielding Institute.

Jantsch, E. (1967). *Technological Forecasting in Perspective.* Paris: OECD.

Jung, C.G. (1938). *Psychology and Religion.* Yale: Yale University Press.

Kervin, J.B. (1992). *Methods for Business Research.* New York: HarperCollins.

Li, X. and Crane, N.B. (1996). *Electronic Styles: A Handbook for Citing Electronic Information.* Medford, N.J: Information Today.

Lockyer, K. and Gordon, J. (1991). *Critical Path Analysis.* London: Pitman.

Lockyer, K. and Gordon, J. (1996). *Project Management and Project Network Techniques.* London: Pitman.

Malinowski, B. (1922). *Argonauts of the Western Pacific.* London: Routledge.

Malinowski, B. (1926). *Crime and Custom in Savage Society.* London: Kegan Paul.

Malinowski, B. (1926). *Magic, Science and Religion., and Other Essays.* Glencoe, Illinois: Free Press.

Malinowski, B. (1926). *Myth in Primitive Psychology.* London: Kegan Paul.

Mead, M. (1928). *Coming of Age in Samoa.* New York: Morrow.

Moccia, P. (1988). A Critique of Compromise: Beyond the Methods Debate, *Advances in Nursing Science,* 10: 1–9.

Morgan, G. (1979). *Response to Mintzberg,* Administrative Science Quarterly, 24(1): 137–9.

Moustakas, C. (1994). *Phenomenological Research Methods.* Thousand Oaks: Sage.

Otley, D. and Berry, A. (1994). Case Study Research in Management Accounting and Control, *Management Accounting Research,* 5: 45–65.

Packer, M.J. (1985). Hermeneutic Inquiry in the Study of Human Conduct, *American Psychologist,* 40: 1081–1093.

Partington, J., Brown. G. and Gordon, G. (1993). *Handbook for External Examiners in Higher Education.* Sheffield: UK Universities' Staff Development Unit and the Universities of Kent and Leeds.

Scapens, R.W. (1990). Researching Management Accounting Practice: The Role of Case Study Methods, *British Accounting Review,* 22: 259–281.

Self, P. (1972). *Administrative Theories and Politics.* London: Allen and Unwin.

Simon, J.L. (1988). *Basic Research Methods in Social Science.* New York: Random House.

Stake, R.E. (1995). *The Art of Case Study Research.* London: Sage.

Susman, G.I. and Evered, R.D. (1978). An Assessment of the Scientific Merits of Action Research, *Administrative Science Quarterly,* Vol. 23, 582–602.

Tashakkori, A. and Teddie, C. (1998). *Mixed Methodology: Combining Qualitative and Quantitative Approaches.* Thousand Oaks: Sage.

Taylor, D.S. (1990). Making the Most of Your Matrices: Hermeneutics, Statistics, and the Repertory Grid, *International Journal for Personal Construct Psychology,* 3, 105–19.

United Kingdom Council for Graduate Education (2002). *Professional Doctorates.* Coventry: UK Council for Graduate Education.

Yin, R.K. (1981). The Case Study Crisis: Some Answers, *Administrative Science Quarterly,* Vol. 26, pp. 58–65.

Yin, R.K. (1994). *Case Study Research: Design and Methods.* Beverly Hills: Sage.

Useful Reference Books

Dictionaries

Allen, R. (ed.) (2004). *Penguin English Dictionary*. London: Penguin.

Brown, L. (ed.) (1993). *The New Shorter Oxford English Dictionary*. Oxford: Clarendon Press.

Collins (2003). *Collins English Dictionary*. Glasgow: Collins.

Collins (2003). *Collins Concise Dictionary and Thesaurus*. Glasgow: Collins.

Collins (2004) *Collins Dictionary and Thesaurus*. Glasgow: Collins.

Chambers (2003). *The Chambers Dictionary*. Edinburgh: Chambers Harrap.

Fowler, H.W., Fowler, F.G. and Pearsall, J. (eds.) (2004). *Concise Oxford English Dictionary*. Oxford: Clarendon Press.

Simpson, J.A. and Weiner, E.S.C. (1989). *Oxford English Dictionary*. Oxford: Clarendon Press.

Soanes, C. and Stevenson, A. (eds.) (2003). *Oxford Dictionary of English*. Oxford: Clarendon Press.

Encyclopaedia

Anderson, T. and McGovern, U. (eds.) (2001). *Chamber's Encyclopaedia*. Edinburgh: Chambers Harrap.

Bahr, L.S., Johnston, B. and Bloomfield, L.A. (1997). *Collier's Encyclopaedia*. New York: P.F. Collier.

Hoiberg, D.H. and Pappas, T.N. (eds.) (2003). *Encyclopaedia Britannica*. London: Encyclopaedia Britannica (UK) Ltd.

Grammar, Spelling and Punctuation

Burt, A. (2004). *Quick Solutions to Common Errors in English.* Oxford: How To Books.

Crystal, D. (2004). *Making Sense of Grammar.* Harlow: Pearson Longman.

Crystal, D. (2004). *Rediscover Grammar.* Harlow: Pearson Longman.

Humphries C. (2003). *Really Simple English Grammar.* Slough: Foulsham.

Leech, G., Cruikshank, R. and Ivanic R. (eds.) (2001). *An A–Z of English Grammar and Usage.* Harlow: Longman.

Strunk, W.I. and White, E.B. (1999). *The Elements of Style.* Harlow: Allyn and Bacon.

Swan, M. (1995). *Practical English Usage.* Oxford: Oxford University Press.

Peck, J. and Coyle, M. (1999). *The Student's Guide to Writing: Grammar, Punctuation and Spelling.* Basingstoke: Palgrave Macmillan.

Waite, M. (ed.) (1995). *Oxford Spelling Dictionary.* Oxford: Clarendon Press.

Quotations

Andrews, R. (ed.) (2003). *The New Penguin Dictionary of Modern Quotations.* Harmondsworth: Penguin.

Knowles, E. (ed.) (2003). *The Concise Oxford Dictionary of Quotations.* Oxford: Oxford University Press.

Knowles, E. (ed.) (2004). *The Oxford Dictionary of Quotations.* Oxford: Oxford University Press.

Ratcliffe, S. (ed.) (2003). *Oxford Quotations By Subject.* Oxford: Oxford University Press.

Synonyms and Antonyms

Hayakawa, S.I. and Fletcher, P.J. (1988). *The Penguin Modern Guide to Synonyms and Related Words*. Harmondsworth: Penguin.

Kipfer, B.A. (2003). *Roget's Descriptive Word Finder: A Dictionary/Thesaurus of Adjectives*. Newton Abbot: Walking Stick Press.

Urdang, L. (ed.) (1991). *Longman Synonym Dictionary*. Harlow: Longman.

Spooner, A. (ed.) (1999). *The Dictionary of Synonyms and Antonyms*. Oxford: Oxford University Press.

Thesauri

Collins (2001) *Collins Paperback Thesaurus*. Glasgow: Collins.

Collins (2002) *Collins Thesaurus A-Z: Complete and Unabridged*. Glasgow: Collins.

Davidson, G. (ed.) (2004) *Roget's Thesaurus of English Words and Phrases*. Harmondsworth: Penguin.

Kahn, J.E. (ed.) (1989). *Reverse Dictionary*. London: Reader's Digest.

Kirkpatrick, E.M. and Waite, M. (eds.) (2001). *The Oxford Paperback Thesaurus*. Oxford: Oxford University Press.

Roget, P. and Davidson, G. (eds.) (2002) *Roget's Thesaurus*. Harmondsworth: Penguin.

Waite, M. (ed.) (2002). *Concise Oxford Thesaurus*. Oxford: Oxford University Press.

Waite, M. (ed.) (2004). *Oxford Thesaurus of English*. Oxford: Oxford University Press.

Sources of Information

American Psychological Association (2002). *Publication Manual.* Washington D.C: American Psychological Association.

Bilboul, R.R. and Kent, F.L. (eds.). (1965–77). *The Retrospective Index to Theses.* Santa Barbara, Calif: American Bibliographical Centre, Clio Press.

(BOPCAS) British Official Publications Current Awareness Service 1995–

Catalogue of British Official Publications Not Published by HMSO 1980–

Chadwyck-Healey's Catalogue of Official Publications Not Published by the Stationery Office.

Chicago Manual of Style (2003). Chicago: University of Chicago Press.

Civil Service Year Book. (biannual). London: The Stationery Office.

Crystal, D. (1998). *The Cambridge Biographical Encyclopaedia.* Cambridge: Cambridge University Press.

General Index to Parliamentary Papers 1852–1990.

HMSO Catalogue 1922–

> *Government Publications* HMSO, 1922–1984
>
> *HMSO Annual Catalogue*, HMSO 1985–1995
>
> *Stationery Office Annual Catalogue* 1996–

Hyams, M. (ed.) (annual). *Index to Theses.* London: Aslib.

Index to British Parliamentary Papers 1801–1922.

Keesing's Record of World Events (formerly Keesing's Contemporary Archives) (monthly). Bristol: Keesing's Publications.

McGovern, U. (ed.) (2002). *Chambers Biographical Dictionary*. Edinburgh: Chambers Harrap.

Munro, D. (1988) *Chambers World Gazetteer*. Edinburgh: Chambers.

Parliamentary Debates (Hansard).

Parliamentary Debates. House of Commons Standing Committees. Official Report.

Subject Catalogue of the House of Commons Parliamentary Papers 1801–1900.

The International Who's Who. London: Europa Publications.

Turner, B. (ed.) (annual). *The Statesman's Yearbook*. Palgrave Macmillan.

(UKOP) UK Official Publications 1980–

Whitaker's Almanac (annual). London: The Stationery Office Books.

Who's Who (annual). London: A&C Black.

Who Was Who

Writers' and Artists' Yearbook (annual). London: A&C Black.

Common Abbreviations

A.D.	anno Domini Lat. ' in the year of our Lord' e.g. A.D. 1066.
anon.	anonymous
app.	appendix
art., arts.	article(s)
assn.	association
b.	born
B.C.	before Christ e.g. 44 B.C.
bibliog.	bibliography
biog.	biography
Bk., Bks.	book(s)
©	copyright e.g. © 2004
c.	circa meaning 'about' as with approximate dates e.g. c. 1507.
cf.	confer Lat. 'compare'
ch., chs.	chapter(s)
Chap, Chaps.	chapter(s)
col., cols.	column(s)
comp.	compiled by
comps.	compilers
cond.	conducted by, conductor
d.	died
dir., dirs.,	directed by, directors
diss.	dissertation

DNB	Dictionary of National Biography
ed., eds.	edited by, editor(s), edition(s) (note: some systems use ed. for edition)
edit., edits.	edition(s)
edn., edns.	edition, editions
e.g.	exempli gratia Lat 'for example'
enl.	enlarged as in 'rev. and enl. ed.'
esp.	especially as in esp. p.331
et al.	et alii Lat 'and others'
et seq.	et sequens, sequential Lat 'and the following'
etc	et cetera Lat 'and so forth'. Not normally employed in dissertation texts
ex., exs.	example(s)
f., ff.	and the following (pages or lines) e.g. pp. 91f. Provide exact references in preference e.g. pp.91-95 rather than pp.91ff
fig., figs.	figures
fol., fols.	folios
front.	frontispiece
ibid.	ibidem Lat 'in the same place' i.e. in the title cited immediately above. not employed in the Harvard system of referencing.
i.e.	id est Lat 'that is'
illus.	illustrated by, illustrator
jour.	journal
Lat.	Latin

l., ll.	Line(s)
L. C.	Library of Congress (note the space between the letters).
loc. cit.	loco citato Lat 'in the place cited'. Not now commonly used
mag.	magazine
ME	Middle English
ms., mss	manuscript(s). A specific manuscript is referred to by Ms.
n., nn.	note(s), usually footnotes
narr., narrs.	narrated by, narrators
N.B.	nota bene Lat 'take notice, mark well'
n.d.	no date (usually in relation to a book when the date of publication is not known)
no., nos.	number(s)
n.p.	no place (of publication of a book). When the location of the publisher is not known. It may also mean no publisher or no page
n. pag.	no pagination
OE	Old English
OED	Oxford English Dictionary
op.	opus (work)
op. cit.	opere citato Lat 'in the work cited'. Not now commonly used
p., pp.	page(s). Not used if preceded by a volume number
par., pars.	paragraph(s)

passim	Lat 'everywhere' i.e. 'throughout the work'
pl., pls.	plate(s)
pref.	preface
prod., prods.	produced by, producer(s)
pseud.	pseudonym
Pt., Pts.	parts
pub.	published by
pubs.	publications
rept., repts.	reported by, report(s)
resp.	respectively e.g. pp. 51,72,89 resp.
rev.	revised, revised by, revision. May sometimes be taken to mean review, or reviewed by, so make this meaning clear by using 'review' if there might be any doubt
rpm.	revolutions per minute
rpt	reprint, reprinted by
sc.	scene
Sec., Secs.	section(s)
sect., sects.	section(s)
ser.	series
sic	Lat 'thus' – often used to call attention to a quoted mistake. It may be put between square brackets when used as an editorial interpolation.
soc.	society
st., sts.	stanza(s)
supp., supps.	supplements

tr.	translated by, translator(s)
trans.	translated by, translator(s)
v., vs.	versus Lat 'against'
v., vv.	verse(s)
vs., vss.	verse(s)
vol., vols.	volume(s)

Useful Websites

It will be appreciated that web sites and their addresses can be changed frequently and at short notice. The following addresses may therefore have changed or no longer be available, but are offered as a starting point for reference.

American Psychological Association. How to Cite Information From the Internet and the World Wide Web

http://www.apa.org/journals/webref.html

Arts and Humanities Research Board

http://www.ahrb.ac.uk

Beckleheimer, J. How Do you Cite URL's in a Bibliography?

http://www.nrlssc.navy.mil/bibliography.html

Biotechnology and Biological Sciences Research Council

http://www.bbrsc.ac.uk

CCTA Government Information Service

http://www.open.gov.uk/index.htm

Classroom Connect, Inc. Citing Internet Addresses

http://www.classroom.com/resource/citingnetresources.asp

Crouse, M. Citing Electronic Information in History Papers

http://www.people.memphis.edu/~mcrouse/elcite.html

Dewey, R.A. APA Style Resources

http://www.psychwww.com/resource/apacrib.htm

Directory of Scholarly and Professional E-Conferences

http://www.n2h2.com/KOVACS

Directory of State and Local Government (US)

http://www.piperinfo.com/state/states

Economic and Social Research Council

http://www.esrc.ac.uk

Engineering and Physical Sciences Research Council

http://www.epsrc.ac.uk

Fletcher, G. and Greenhill, A. Academic Referencing of Internet-based Resources

http://spaceless.com/WWWVL/refs.html

Harnack, A. and Kleppinger, G. Beyond the MLA Handbook: Documenting Electronic Sources on the Internet.

Infoseek Net Search

http://www2.infoseek.com/Query

http://english.ttu.edu/kairos/1.2/inbox/mla.html

International Address Finders

http://www.worldmail.com/wedemail.com/wede4e

http://www.iaft.net

International Organisation for Standardisation (ISO). Excerpts from ISO Draft International Standard 690-2- Information and documentation- Bibliographic references- Electronic documents or parts thereof

http://www.nlc-bnc.ca/iso/tc46sc9/standard/690-2e.htm

Internet Book Shop

http://www.bookshop.co.uk/

Internet Scout Project

http://wwwscout.cs.wisc.edu

Land T. Web Extension to American Psychological Association Style (WEAPAS)

(Proposed standard for referencing online documents in scientific publications)

http://www.beadsland.com/weapas/

Li, X. and Crane, N. (1995). Bibliographic Formats for Citing Electronic Information.

http://www.uvm.edu/~xli/reference/estyles.html

Medical Research Council

http://www.mrc.ac.uk

Modern Language Association (MLA) MLA Style

http://www.mla.org/main_stl-nf.htm

National Postgraduate Committee (UK)

http://www.npc.org.uki

Natural Environment Research Council

http://www.nerc.ac.uk

Page, M.E. A Brief Citation Guide for Internet Sources in History and the Humanities

http://h-net2.msu.edu/%7Eafrica/citation.html

Particle Physics and Astronomy Research Council

http://www.pparc.ac.uk

Peoplesearch

http://www.w3com.com/psearch

Public Records Office (UK)

http://pro.gov.uk

Publishers' catalogues

http://lights.com/publisher

Publishers' details

http://www.bic.org.uk.bic/publish.html

Purdue University. MLA Format: Giving Credit To Sources

http://owl.english.purdue.edu/handouts/research/r_apa.html

Research Councils (UK) gateway

http://www.rresearch-councils.ac.uk

Tent, J. et al. Citing E-text Summary (LINGUIST list).

http://www.emich.edu/%7Elinguist/issues/6/6-210.html

The World Wide Web United Nations

http://wwwundcp.or.at/unlinks.html

University of Alberta. Citation Style Guides for Internet and Electronic Sources.

http://www.library.ualberta.ca/guides/citation/index.cfm

Wainwright, M. Citation Style for Internet Sources.

http://www.cl.cam.ac.uk/users/maw13/citation.html

Walker, J. Columbia Online Style: MLA-Style Citations of Electronic Sources.

http://www.cas.usf.edu/english/walker/mla.html

WebCrawler Searching

http://webcrawler.com/

Index